Book Title: A Recommendation for the Use of PIV Credentials in Physical Access Control Systems (PACS)

Book Author: William I. MacGregor; Ketan L. Mehta; David A. Cooper; Karen A. Scarfone

Book Abstract: This document provides best practice guidelines for integrating the PIV Card with the physical access control systems (PACS) that authenticate the cardholders in Federal facilities. Specifically, this document recommends a risk-based approach for selecting appropriate PIV authentication mechanisms to manage physical access to Federal government facilities and assets. This document also proposes a PIV implementation maturity model to measure the progress of facility and agency implementations.

Citation: NIST SP - 800-116

Keyword: HSPD-12; PIV; PACS; FIPS 201; PIV authentication mechanisms; Smart Card

NIST Special Publication 800-116

A Recommendation for the Use of PIV Credentials in Physical Access Control Systems (PACS)

National Institute of
Standards and Technology
U.S. Department of Commerce

William MacGregor
Ketan Mehta
David Cooper
Karen Scarfone

INFORMATION SECURITY

Computer Security Division
Information Technology Laboratory
National Institute of Standards and Technology
Gaithersburg, MD, 20899-8930

November 2008

U.S. Department of Commerce
Carlos M. Gutierrez, Secretary

National Institute of Standards and Technology
Patrick D. Gallagher, Deputy Director

REPORTS ON COMPUTER SYSTEMS TECHNOLOGY

The Information Technology Laboratory (ITL) at the National Institute of Standards and Technology (NIST) promotes the U.S. economy and public welfare by providing technical leadership for the Nation's measurement and standards infrastructure. ITL develops tests, test methods, reference data, proof of concept implementations, and technical analyses to advance the development and productive use of information technology. ITL's responsibilities include the development of management, administrative, technical, and physical standards and guidelines for the cost-effective security and privacy of non-national security-related information in Federal information systems. This Special Publication 800-series reports on ITL's research, guidelines, and outreach efforts in information system security, and its collaborative activities with industry, government, and academic organizations.

National Institute of Standards and Technology Special Publication 800-116, 71 pages

(November 2008)

Acknowledgements

The authors, David Cooper, William MacGregor, and Karen Scarfone of the National Institute of Standards and Technology (NIST) and Ketan Mehta of Mehta, Inc., wish to thank their colleagues who reviewed drafts of this document and contributed to its development. We thank Tony Cieri and Ron Martin for substantial written contributions to the document. The authors gratefully acknowledge and appreciate the support received from the Interagency Security Committee, Department of Justice (DOJ), General Services Administration (GSA), Department of Homeland Security (DHS), Department of Defense (DoD), Social Security Administration (SSA), and Department of Treasury in developing this document. Special thanks to our expert collaborators who participated in weekly conference calls and provided comments on many versions of the document:

+ Tim Baldridge

+ Magdalena Benitez

+ Joe Broghamer

+ Mike Defrancisco

+ Hildegard Ferraiolo

+ Scott Glaser

+ Christopher Hernandez

+ Gwainevere Hess

+ Everett Hilliard

+ Nolin Huddleston

+ Lemar Jones

+ C. Larson

+ Edward Layo

+ Diana Londergan

+ Ron Martin

+ Eric Mitchell

+ Steve Mitchell

+ Benjamin Overbey

+ Ron Ross

+ Austin Smith

+ Carlton Stevenson

+ David Vanderweele

+ Tom Whittle

+ Craig Zeigler

Table of Contents

List of Figures

List of Tables

1.   Executive Summary

The physical access control systems (PACS) deployed in most Federal buildings are facility-centric rather than enterprise-centric and utilize proprietary PACS architectures. Therefore, many issued identification (ID) cards operate only with the PACS for which they were issued. The technologies used in these systems may offer little or no authentication assurance, because the issued ID cards are easily cloned or counterfeited. In addition to the lack of interoperability, deployed PACS technology presents the following challenges:

+   Scalability. Some deployed systems are limited in their capability to process the longer credential numbers necessary for Government-wide interoperability.

+   Security. Deployed PACS readers can read an identifying number from a card, but in most cases they do not perform a cryptographic challenge/response exchange. Most bar code, magnetic stripe, and proximity cards can be copied easily. The technologies used in these systems may offer little or no authentication assurance.

+   Validity. Deployed PACS control expiration of credentials through an expiration date stored in a site database. There is no simple way to synchronize the expiration or revocation of credentials for a Federal employee or contractor across multiple sites.

+   Efficiency. Use of personal identification numbers (PIN), public key infrastructure, and biometrics with deployed PACS is managed on a site-specific basis. Individuals must enroll PINs, keys, and biometrics at each site. Since PINs, keys, and biometrics are often stored in a site database, they may not be technically interoperable with PACS at other sites.

Homeland Security Presidential Directive 12 (HSPD-12) sets a clear goal to improve PACS through the use of government-wide standards. [HSPD-12] Federal Information Processing Standard 201 (FIPS 201) defines characteristics of the identity credential that can be interoperable government-wide. [FIPS201] In the context of HSPD-12, the term *interoperability* means the ability to use any Personal Identity Verification (PIV) Card with any application performing one or more PIV authentication mechanisms. FIPS 201 defines authentication mechanisms at three E-Authentication assurance levels (SOME, HIGH, and VERY HIGH), and standardizes optional credential elements that extend trust in the PIV System to functions beyond authentication. A gap remains, however, between the concepts of authentication assurance levels and their application in a PACS environment. To close this gap, this document:

+   Discusses the different PIV Card capabilities so that the risk-based assessment can be aligned with the appropriate PIV authentication mechanism.

+   Introduces the concept of "Controlled, Limited, Exclusion" areas to employ risk-based PIV authentication mechanisms for different areas within a facility.

+   Proposes a PIV Implementation Maturity Model (PIMM) to measure the progress of facility and agency implementations.

+   Recommends to Federal agencies an overall strategy for the implementation of PIV authentication mechanisms with agency facility PACS.

Since the areas accessible via different access points within a facility do not all have the same security requirement, the PIV authentication mechanisms should be selected to be consistent with, and integral to, the overall security requirements of the protected area. A given facility may need multiple authentication mechanisms. Therefore, the designation of "Controlled, Limited, Exclusion" areas, detailed in Section 7.3, is applied to the protected area. Specifically, this document recommends PIV authentication mechanisms for "Controlled, Limited, Exclusion" in terms of authentication factors as shown in Table 1-1.

Table 1-1. Authentication Factors for Security Areas

Security Areas	Number of Authentication Factors Required
Controlled 1	
Limited 2	
Exclusion 3	

PIV authentication mechanisms should be implemented in accordance with Table 1-1. Figure 1-1 illustrates the innermost perimeter at which each PIV authentication mechanism may be used based on the authentication assurance level of the mechanism. The combined effect of Table 1-1 and Figure 1-1 determines exactly what mechanisms may be used. (See Section 7.3) An exhaustive list of possible uses of PIV authentication mechanisms against protected areas is provided in Appendix C.

Visual (VIS), Cardholder Unique Identifier (CHUID), Biometric (BIO), Attended Biometric (BIO-A), and PIV Authentication Key (PKI) are PIV authentication mechanisms defined in FIPS 201 and described in Section 3. Card Authentication Key (CAK) is an optional PIV authentication mechanism that is described in Section 3.

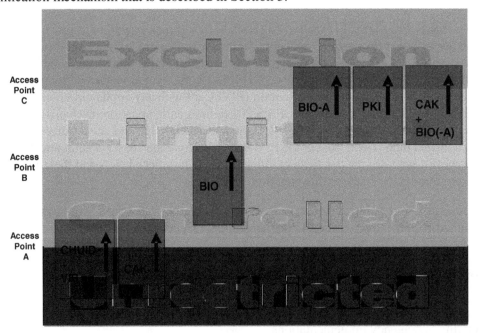

Figure 1-1: Innermost Use of PIV Authentication Mechanisms

A risk-based migration strategy should be planned and implemented to achieve PIV enabling. This document recommends a model that allows agencies to incrementally PIV-enable access points. The model is defined in terms of maturity levels as follows:

+ Maturity Level 1—Ad hoc PIV verification.

+ Maturity Level 2—Systematic PIV verification to Controlled areas. PIV Cards and currently deployed non-PIV PACS cards are accepted for access to the Controlled areas at this level.

+ Maturity Level 3—Access to Exclusion areas by PIV or exception only. Non-PIV PACS cards are not accepted for access to the Exclusion areas at this level.

+ Maturity Level 4—Access to Limited areas by PIV or exception only. Non-PIV PACS cards are not accepted for access to the Limited or Exclusion areas at this level.

+ Maturity Level 5—Access to Controlled areas by PIV or exception only. Non-PIV PACS cards are not accepted for access to any areas at this level.

2.   Introduction

2.1   Authority

This document has been developed by the National Institute of Standards and Technology (NIST) to further its statutory responsibilities under the Federal Information Security Management Act (FISMA) of 2002, P.L. 107-347. NIST is responsible for developing standards and guidelines, including minimum requirements, for providing adequate information security for all agency operations and assets, but such standards and guidelines shall not apply to national security systems. This guideline is consistent with the requirements of the Office of Management and Budget (OMB) Circular A-130, Section 8b(3), Securing Agency Information Systems, as analyzed in A-130, Appendix IV: Analysis of Key Sections. Supplemental information is provided in A-130, Appendix III.

This guideline has been prepared for use by Federal agencies. It may also be used by nongovernmental organizations on a voluntary basis and is not subject to copyright. (Attribution would be appreciated by NIST.)

Nothing in this document should be taken to contradict standards and guidelines made mandatory and binding on Federal agencies by the Secretary of Commerce under statutory authority.[1] Nor should these guidelines be interpreted as altering or superseding the existing authorities of the Secretary of Commerce, Director of the OMB, or any other Federal official.

2.2   Background

HSPD-12 mandates the establishment of a government-wide standard for identity credentials to improve physical security in Federally controlled facilities[2]. To that end, HSPD-12 requires all government employees and contractors be issued a new identity credential based on the FIPS 201 on PIV. Following FIPS 201, this credential is referred to herein as a PIV Card[3].

HSPD-12 explicitly requires the use of PIV Cards "in gaining physical access to Federally controlled facilities and logical access to Federally controlled information systems." [HSPD-12] The PIV Card employs microprocessor-based smart card technology, and is designed to be counterfeit-resistant, tamper-resistant, and interoperable across Federal government facilities. Additionally, the FIPS 201 standards suite defines the authentication mechanisms as transactions between a PIV Card and a relying party. FIPS 201 does not, however, elaborate on the uses and applications of the PIV Card. This document provides guidelines on the uses of PIV Cards with PACS.

The PACS technologies deployed in most Federal buildings are facility-centric rather than enterprise-centric and utilize proprietary PACS architectures. Historically, a security advantage was seen in not having the design of the security system published or readily accommodating substitution. For this and other reasons, many deployed PACS are not interoperable. Moreover,

---

[1] In particular, whenever a PACS uses cryptographic mechanisms, FIPS 140-2 and NIST SP 800-57 may apply.

[2] Federally controlled facilities as defined in Section 1D of OMB Memorandum M-05-24.
http://www.whitehouse.gov/omb/memoranda/fy2005/m05-24.pdf

[3] Federal agencies may refer to PIV Cards by other names, for example, "identity badges" or "access cards". In this document, all such credentials issued by an accredited PIV Card Issuer are called PIV Cards.

lack of agency card technology standards and current credential numbering systems are the factors that limit interoperability across agencies. In other words, an identity credential issued by one PACS may not have the capability to be used by another. To enhance security and promote interoperability, it is essential to develop an efficient and cost-effective strategy to migrate PACS to standardized methods as defined in FIPS 201. The application of cryptographic authentication and integrity methods allows the security of authentication to be improved, the design of authentication to rely on open standards, and the need for secrecy regarding authentication to be concentrated on cryptographic keys.

Full compliance with HSPD-12, and the use of PIV authentication mechanisms for access to Federal facilities and systems as required by HSPD-12, should be the principal goals of a department or agency implementation plan. Recognizing that implementation will take time, migration goals and plans should be developed to PIV-enable PACS installations, while meeting continuity of operations and resource constraints. Plans may include change management strategies such as:

+ The use of "multi-technology" readers, enabling a transition to the PIV-enabled PACS over time by allowing proprietary identity cards and PIV Cards to work side-by-side.

+ Retrofit or upgrade the existing PACS to use PIV Cards.

+ Coexistence of PIV-enabled and existing PACS in leased multi-tenant facilities.

   Recommendation: The OMB Memorandum [M-08-01] requires that the credential issuance be accomplished by October 27, 2008 (or by the date specified in the implementation plan mutually agreed-upon by the agency and OMB). Agency implementation plans should be written to accomplish the goals of HSPD-12.

2.3 Purpose and Scope

The purpose of this document is to describe a strategy allowing agencies to PIV-enable their PACS, and migrate to government-wide interoperability. Specifically, the document recommends a risk-based approach for selecting appropriate PIV authentication mechanisms to manage physical access to Federal government facilities and assets. With the intent to facilitate and encourage greater use of PIV Cards, this document:

+ Describes the desired characteristics of a target implementation of PIV-enabled PACS.

+ Describes trust and infrastructure challenges that must be overcome to achieve government-wide credential interoperability.

+ Discusses the PIV Card capabilities so that risk-based assessment can be aligned with the appropriate PIV authentication mechanism.

+ Recommends to Federal agencies an overall strategy for the implementation of PIV authentication mechanisms with agency facility PACS.

+ Proposes a PIMM to measure the progress of facility and agency implementations.

As stated above, this document focuses on the use of PIV Cards to gain access to Federal buildings and facilities. This document does not address non-PIV authentication mechanisms.

Although the ergonomic design of PACS components is outside the scope of this publication, the 1998 Amendment to Section 508 of the Rehabilitation Act has special relevance to PACS components. [SECTION508] PACS access controls are intended to be unavoidable. Section 508 should be considered early during projects that integrate the PIV System with PACS. Section 508 should be considered as it applies to enrollment software, smart card and biometric readers, monitoring systems, and access control point sensors and actuators. Note that FIPS 201, Section 4.4.1, states that an alternative to BIO or BIO-A authentication mechanism should be used if one or more fingers cannot be enrolled. Further information can be found at [SECTION508], in [FIPS201], and in [SP800-76].

Many other aspects of physical access control are outside the scope of this publication. Authorization (i.e., granting permission within a PACS for an identified person to pass access control points) is a critical security function, but is out of scope for the PIV System. Other out-of-scope functions include area protection, intrusion detection, monitoring and tracking (other than at access control points), and enforcement of access control decisions. It is understood that PACS may also be integrated with surveillance systems, fire control systems, evacuation systems, etc., within a facility. This document does not address the integration of PACS with other facility-centric information technology (IT) systems, although it has been written to minimize conflicts during such integration. Therefore, if the integration of the measures outlined in this document creates a life-safety risk, organizations will need to mitigate these risks before applying the measures.

The evaluation of specific PACS architectures or implementations is also outside the scope of this publication, as is the standardization of PACS. The creation of specific migration plans for each agency and facility is also not the intent of this document, although it offers advice on the construction of such plans. Unless normatively referenced, this document is a best practice guideline.

> **Recommendation:** This document recommends a risk-based approach for selecting appropriate PIV authentication mechanisms to manage physical access to Federal government facilities and assets. Agencies should seek recommendations on PACS architectures, authorization, and facility protection from other sources.

2.4 Audience

This document is intended for the government officials responsible for implementing HSPD-12. This document will also aid government executives (i.e., decision makers) to evaluate business cases and develop strategies for their departments or agencies. Information in this document is also useful to the government contractors and security industry vendors implementing HSPD-12-related systems, products, and services.

3.   Terminology

The following terms are used in this document and are not defined in FIPS 201.

Access Control: A function or a system that restricts access to authorized persons only.

Access Control List: A list of (identifier, permissions) pairs associated with a resource or an asset. As an expression of security policy, a person may perform an operation on a resource or asset if and only if the person's identifier is present in the access control list (explicitly or implicitly), and the permissions in the (identifier, permissions) pair include the permission to perform the requested operation.

Assurance Level (or **E-Authentication Assurance Level**): A measure of trust or confidence in an authentication mechanism defined in OMB Memorandum M-04-04 and NIST Special Publication (SP) 800-63, in terms of four levels: [M-04-04]

- Level 1: LITTLE OR NO confidence
- Level 2: SOME confidence
- Level 3: HIGH confidence
- Level 4: VERY HIGH confidence

Authentication: A process that establishes the origin of information, or determines an entity's identity. In this publication, authentication often means the performance of a PIV authentication mechanism.

Authentication in Context: Authentication in context is a concept in which PACS may benefit from previous authentication within nested areas in a facility. The PACS may use information from previous access control decisions ("context") when making a new access control decision.

Authorization: In this publication, a process that associates permission to access a resource or asset with a person and the person's identifier(s).

Authenticator: A memory, possession, or quality of a person that can serve as proof of identity, when presented to a verifier of the appropriate kind. For example, passwords, cryptographic keys, and fingerprints are authenticators.

BIO or BIO-A: A FIPS 201 authentication mechanism that is implemented by using a Fingerprint data object sent from the PIV Card to the PACS. Note that the short-hand "BIO (-A)" is used throughout the document to represent both BIO and BIO-A authentication mechanisms.

Biometric: An authenticator produced from measurable qualities of a living person.

Building Security Committee: A committee consisting of representatives of Federal tenants in a facility, and possibly the building owner or management. The committee is responsible for building-specific security issues and approval of security policies and practices.

Card Authentication Key (CAK): A PIV authentication mechanism (or the PIV Card key of the same name) that is implemented by an asymmetric or symmetric key challenge/response protocol. The CAK is an optional mechanism defined in NIST SP 800-73. [SP800-73] NIST strongly recommends that every PIV Card contain an asymmetric CAK and corresponding certificate, and that agencies use the asymmetric CAK protocol, rather than a symmetric CAK protocol, whenever the CAK authentication mechanism is used with PACS. See Section 7.1.4.

Cardholder Unique Identifier (CHUID): A FIPS 201 authentication mechanism that is implemented by transmission of the CHUID data object from the PIV Card to PACS, or the PIV Card data object of the same name.

Certificate: A data object containing a subject identifier, a public key, and other information, that is digitally signed by a Certification Authority. Certificates convey trust in the relationship of the subject identifier to the public key.

Cloning: In this publication, a process to create a verbatim copy of a PIV Card, or a partial copy sufficient to perform one or more authentication mechanisms as if it were the original card.

Contact Reader: A smart card reader that communicates with the Integrated Circuit chip in a smart card using electrical signals on wires touching the smart card's contact pad. The PIV contact interface is standardized by International Organization of Standards / International Electrotechnical Commission (ISO/IEC) 7816-3. [ISO/IEC7816]

Contactless Reader: A smart card reader that communicates with the Integrated Circuit chip in a smart card using radio frequency (RF) signaling. The PIV contactless interface is standardized by ISO/IEC 14443. [ISO/IEC14443]

Controller (or **Control Panel,** or **Panel**): A device located within the secure area that communicates with multiple PIV Card readers and door actuators, and with the Head End System. The PIV Card readers provide cardholder information to the Controller, which it uses to make access control decisions and release door locking mechanisms. The Controller communicates with the Head End System to receive changes in access permissions, report unauthorized access attempts and send audit records and other log information. Most modern controllers can continue to operate properly during periods of time in which communication with the Head End is disrupted and can journal transactions so that they can be reported to the Head End when communication is restored.

Counterfeiting: In this publication, the creation of a fake ID card that can perform one or more authentication mechanisms, without copying a legitimate card (see **Cloning**).

Credential: In this publication, a collection of information about a person, attested to by an issuing authority. A credential may be a physical artifact (e.g., a **PIV Card**) or a data object (e.g., a **certificate**). One or more data object credentials may be stored on the same physical memory device (e.g., a smart card).

Credential Validation: The process of determining if a credential is *valid*, i.e., it was legitimately issued, its activation date has been reached, it has not expired, it has not been tampered with, and it has not been terminated, suspended, or revoked by the issuing authority.

Digital Signature: A data object produced by a digital signature method, such as Rivest, Shamir, Aldeman (RSA) or the Elliptic Curve Digital Signature Algorithm (ECDSA), that when verified provides strong evidence of the origin and integrity of the signed data object.

Federal Agency Smart Credential Number (FASC-N): As required by FIPS 201, the primary identifier on the PIV Card for physical access control. The FASC-N is a fixed length (25 byte) data object, specified in [TIG SCEPACS], and included in several data objects on a PIV Card.

FASC-N Identifier: The FASC-N shall be in accordance with [TIG SCEPACS]. A subset of FASC-N, a FASC-N Identifier, is a unique identifier as described in [TIG SCEPACS]. Section 2.1, 10th paragraph of [TIG SCEPACS] states "For full interoperability of a PACS it must at a minimum be able to distinguish fourteen digits (i.e., a combination of an Agency Code, System Code, and Credential Number) when matching FASC-N based credentials to enrolled card holders." Also, Section 6.6, 3rd paragraph of [TIG SCEPACS] states, "The combination of an Agency Code, System Code, and Credential Number is a fully qualified number that is uniquely assigned to a single individual". The Agency Code is assigned to each Department or Agency by Special Publication 800-87, *Codes for the Identification of Federal and Federally-Assisted Organizations* [SP800-87]. The subordinate System Code and Credential Number value assignment is subject to Department or Agency policy, provided that the FASC-N Identifier (i.e. the concatenated Agency Code, System Code, and Credential Number) is unique for each card.

Head End System (or **Access Control Server**): A system including application software, database, a Head End server, and one or more networked personal computers. The Head End server is typically used to enroll an individual's name, create a unique ID number, and assign access privileges and an expiration date. The server is also used to maintain this information and refresh the Controller(s) with the latest changes.

Identifier (or **Unique Identifier**): In this publication, a data object, assigned by an authority, that unambiguously identifies a person within a defined community. For example, a Driver License number identifies a licensed driver within a State. The authority registers people and guarantees assignment of each identifier to a unique person.

Identity Credential: A **credential** that contains one or more identifiers for its subject, a person. In this publication, an identity credential is designed to verify the identity of its subject through **authentication mechanisms**, either manually (see **VIS**) or electronically (see **CHUID**, **CAK**, **PKI**, **BIO**, and **BIO-A**).

Infrastructure: Distributed substructure of a large-scale organization that facilitates related functions or operations, e.g., telecommunications infrastructure. With regard to PACS, components include conduit, cabling, power supplies, battery backup, electrified door hardware, door position switches, and remote exit devices, as well as connectivity with other life safety systems that will ensure egress in the event of an emergency.

Interoperability: In this publication, the quality of allowing any government facility or information system to verify a cardholder's identity using the credentials on the PIV Card, regardless of the PIV Card Issuer (PCI).

Issuance (or **Credential Issuance**): The process by which an issuing authority obtains and verifies information about a person, assigns one or more unique identifiers to the person, prepares information to be placed in or on a credential, produces a physical or data object credential, and delivers the finished credential to its subject. In the case of PIV Cards, issuance is performed only by accredited PCIs.

Multi-Factor Authentication: Authentication based on more than one factor. In some contexts, each factor is a different authenticator. In other contexts, each factor is one of "something you know, something you have, something you are" (i.e., memorized fact, token, or biometric) and thus the number of factors is 1, 2, or 3.

PACS Registration: The process of authenticating, validating, and verifying information about the PIV cardholder prior to entering the information into a PACS server. The information added during registration is then utilized to perform authentication and authorization of an individual at an access point.

Path Validation (or **Trust Path Validation**): The process of verifying the binding between the subject identifier and subject public key in a certificate, based on the public key of a trust anchor, through the validation of a chain of certificates that begins with a certificate issued by the trust anchor and ends with the target certificate. Successful path validation provides strong evidence that the information in the target certificate is trustworthy.

Personal Identification Number (PIN): Typically, a short numeric password (4 to 8 digits) used as an authenticator with a bank card, ID card, or other personal security device.

Personal Identity Verification (PIV) Card: The identity credential mandated by HSPD-12 and defined by FIPS 201 as an end-point PIV Card. A PIV Card is a smart card with contact and contactless communication capability, and eleven defined data objects for interoperability, five mandatory and six optional.

PIV Implementation Maturity Model (PIMM): PIMM is a PIV implementation maturity model that can be used to measure the progress of a facility or an agency towards accepting PIV Card.

PIV System: A system comprised of components and processes that support a common (smart card-based) platform for identity authentication across Federal departments and agencies for access to multiple types of physical access environments.

Physical Access Control System (PACS): An electronic system that controls the ability of people or vehicles to enter a protected area, by means of authentication and authorization at access control points.

PKI: For this document, a PIV authentication mechanism that is implemented by an asymmetric PIV authentication key challenge/response protocol.

Private Key: A cryptographic key used with a public key cryptographic algorithm, which is uniquely associated with an entity, and not made public; it is used to generate a digital signature; this key is mathematically linked with a corresponding public key.

Public Key: A cryptographic key used with a public key cryptographic algorithm, uniquely associated with an entity, and which may be made public; it is used to verify a digital signature; this key is mathematically linked with a corresponding private key.

Reader: A device that interfaces with a PIV Card and a Controller to execute or support execution of one or more PIV authentication mechanisms.

Relying Party: In this publication, an entity, such as a PACS, that depends upon the trust model of the PIV System to correctly produce the results of authentication, i.e., the identity of the cardholder.

Revocation: The process by which an issuing authority renders an issued credential useless. For example, a Certification Authority may revoke certificates it issues. Typically, a certificate is revoked if its corresponding private key is known to be, or suspected to be, compromised, or if the certificate's subject affiliation is changed.

Secret Key: A key used by a symmetric key algorithm to encrypt, decrypt, sign, or verify information. In a Symmetric Key Infrastructure (SKI), the sender and receiver of encrypted information must share the same secret key.

Skimming: Surreptitiously obtaining data from a contactless smart card, using a hidden reader that powers, commands, and reads from the card within the maximum read distance (reported as about 25 cm with ISO/IEC 14443 smart cards like the PIV Card). [SKIMMER]

Sniffing: Surreptitiously obtaining data from a contactless smart card, using a hidden reader that receives RF signals from a legitimate reader and smart card when they perform a transaction. Sniffing is a form of electronic eavesdropping. Sniffing is possible at greater distances than skimming.

Social Engineering: A process or technique, similar to a confidence game, used to obtain information from a person without raising suspicion.

Termination: In this publication, the action of an identity credential issuer that causes the credential to become invalid.

Trust Anchor: A named entity producing digital signatures, and a corresponding certificate that a relying party has decided to trust, i.e., if a digital signature is verified using the public key within the certificate, the signature is trusted to have been made by the entity named in the certificate.

VIS: A FIPS 201 authentication mechanism in which the visual identity verification of a PIV Card is done by a human guard.

Validation: In this publication, the process of determining that an identity credential was legitimately issued and is still valid, i.e., has not expired or been terminated.

Verification: The process of determining if an assertion is true, particularly the process of determining if a data object possesses a digital signature produced by the purported signer.

Wiegand: With regard to deployed PACS, a one-way communication protocol consisting of a formatted bit string used from the access reader to the Controller. It can be used with any media, including proximity, bar code, magnetic stripe, and smart cards.

4.   Threat Environment

The PIV System is intended to enhance security and trust in identity credentials, but no practical system can guarantee perfect security. This section discusses known technical threats to PIV authentication mechanisms, especially the CHUID authentication mechanism. Methods of attack are described in general terms, and this is not an exhaustive list of possible attacks. Attackers often succeed by exploiting overlooked or newly introduced vulnerabilities in operational systems.

The PIV System protects the trustworthiness of the PIV Card data objects through PIV Card access rules and digital signatures. Overall trust in the execution of a PIV authentication mechanism is also dependent on correct operation of the PIV Card, the PACS, and the PIV Card validation infrastructure, and, to a degree, on protecting the confidentiality, integrity, and availability of the communication channels among them. Attacks may, therefore, be directed against any of these components, with varying difficulty and potential impact.

The factors critical to sustained trust in the PIV System are:

+   The strength of cryptographic operations

+   The protection of private and secret keys by system components

+   The successful decryption and/or signature verification of data objects at expected times

+   The continuous implementation of access rules by the PIV Card

+   The dependable operation of other system elements in the PIV System and the PACS.

To execute a PIV authentication mechanism, the PIV cardholder presents his or her card to the PACS. The presentation of the PIV Card occurs outside the security perimeter to which access is requested. When the presentation occurs at the outermost perimeter of a facility, the cardholder is in an Unrestricted area, and various technical attacks on PACS are easily carried out. Special security precautions must be taken to ensure protection of these devices at the outermost perimeters of the facility. Even at interior perimeters, the degree of protection provided by enclosing perimeters may be modest when the means of attack can be easily concealed. Possible attack vectors include identifier collisions, terminated PIV Cards, visual counterfeiting, skimming, sniffing, social engineering, electronic cloning, and electronic counterfeiting. These methods of attack, as well as others, are discussed below.

4.1   Identifier Collisions

By definition, a unique identifier for a PIV Card is a data artifact with a fixed value unique to one particular PIV Card. PCIs create unique identifiers during the card issuance process. The presence of a unique identifier allows a PIV Card to be uniquely identified by a relying system, such as a PACS. If the unique identifier is ever truncated, compressed, hashed, or modified, information could be lost. If information is lost from the unique identifier before it is compared against Access Control List (ACL) entries, multiple cards may generate the same reduced identifier. This is called an *identifier collision*. A collision means that multiple PIV Cards will appear to belong to the same person, and will all be granted the same access privileges.

The PIV Card mitigates the risk of collision by defining a unique FASC-N Identifier for the purposes of physical access control decisions. To prevent collisions, all access control decisions should be made by comparing the 14 decimal digit FASC-N Identifier, and optionally the values of additional FASC-N fields, against the ACL entries. See Appendix B for details and examples.

4.2   Terminated PIV Cards

PIV Cards may be terminated for a number of reasons, including a lost or stolen card. A terminated PIV Card could continue to open doors with the CHUID authentication mechanism long after the card has been terminated. As described in FIPS 201, the check for termination should be performed by a status check, using either the Online Certificate Status Protocol (OCSP) or Certificate Revocation Lists (CRL), on a PIV authentication certificate. Credential validation is required by FIPS 201 for the PKI authentication mechanism, but it is not required, nor described, for the CHUID authentication mechanism. If a PIV Card is reported as lost and then terminated by the issuer, PACS relying on CHUID authentication mechanism will continue to accept the CHUID until the user is de-authorized in each of those systems. If a PACS caches the status of PIV Cards, the cached status of a terminated PIV Card will remain "valid" until the cache is refreshed. The process for PACS de-authorization is not required or defined by FIPS 201, raising the possibility that on-line credential validation will not be implemented, or not effectively implemented, where the CHUID authentication mechanism is employed.

The PIV System mitigates the risk of use of a misappropriated PIV Card (which has been successfully reported and revoked) through the process of on-line credential validation. FIPS 201 Section 5.4.5 equates on-line PIV credential validation to path validation of a PIV authentication certificate. In the CHUID authentication mechanism, only the CHUID data object is read from the PIV Card, and a reader cannot check the status of a PIV authentication certificate on the basis of the CHUID alone. Therefore, it is recommended that path validation of a PIV authentication certificate be done at PIV registration, and periodically repeated by the PACS server as long as registration is maintained. Implementation methods are further discussed in Sections 7.4 and 7.5.

4.3   Visual Counterfeiting

PIV Cards are used in the VIS authentication mechanism that requires visual inspection of the PIV Card by a security guard. A visual counterfeit mimics the appearance, but not the electronic behavior, of an actual PIV Card. A PIV replica may be created by color photocopying or graphic illustration methods and color printing to blank stock. Because of the required presence of one or more security features on the PIV Card, a visual counterfeit is unlikely to pass close examination, provided guards are trained to recognize security features. ID cards may receive only cursory examination when used as "flash passes", however.

The PIV Card mitigates the risk of visual counterfeiting through its capability for rapid electronic authentication, and to a lesser degree, by the presence of one or more security features on the surface of the card. Given the ready availability of high-quality scanners, graphic editing software, card stock, and smart card printers, electronic verification is strongly recommended, either in place of the VIS authentication mechanism or in combination with it.

4.4   Skimming

A contactless PIV Card reader with a sensitive antenna can be concealed in a briefcase, and is capable of reading ISO/IEC 14443 contactless smart cards like the PIV Card at a distance of at least 25 cm, as demonstrated in [SKIMMER]. The range of a skimmer is limited primarily by the requirement for the skimmer to supply power to the PIV Card by inductive coupling. A concealed skimmer could immediately obtain the free-read data from the PIV Card, which includes the CHUID[4] and the certificates.

> *The PIV Card mitigates the risk of skimming by access rules that prevent the release of biometric and other data over the contactless interface, and by minimizing content in the free-read data objects. Additional protection can be achieved by shielding techniques that positively deactivate a PIV Card when not in use. The electromagnetically opaque sleeve mentioned in FIPS 201 Section 2.4 is one such technique.*

4.5   Sniffing

When a PIV Card is presented to a contactless reader at an access point, the reader supplies power to the PIV Card through inductive coupling and a series of messages is exchanged between the PIV Card and reader using RF communications. A sniffer is a receiver that does not supply power to the smart card. A sniffer can operate at greater distance than a skimmer (sniffing at a distance of about 10 m has been reported), because a legitimate reader powers the PIV Card at the nominal distance of a few centimeters, while the sniffer's RF receiver is farther away. Potentially, a sniffer could capture the entire message transaction between the contactless reader and the PIV Card.

> *The PIV Card mitigates the risk of sniffing by the same access rules that prevent the release of biometric and other data over the contactless interface. The CHUID can be sniffed, however, when used over a contactless interface. Shielding techniques that positively deactivate a PIV Card when not in use cannot mitigate the risk of sniffing, because a PIV Card must be activated to perform a legitimate authentication transaction.*

4.6   Social Engineering

If an attacker persuaded the cardholder to give them possession of the PIV Card, the attacker could quickly insert the card into a contact reader and copy all of the information available as free-read (the CHUID, the security object, the Card Capability Container, and the certificates) over the contact interface. An attacker could also attempt a remote attack similar to well-known phishing attacks by creating a web page that asks the subject to "insert their PIV Card and enter their PIN" for an apparently legitimate purpose. If the cardholder complies, under some assumptions the attacker could capture the cardholder's PIN and all of the readable PIV data objects, including the CHUID.

> *The PIV Card mitigates the risk of social engineering attacks by blocking the release of all private and secret keys, and by requiring two-factor authentication (PIV Card and PIN) to perform cryptographic operations with the PIV Authentication Key. Moreover, the PIV Card is blocked upon exceeding the allocated number of bad PIN tries. Additional technical and procedural controls may be needed to counter PIV phishing.*

---

[4] CHUID is one of the data elements of PIV credentials that uniquely identifies the PIV cardholder. CHUID stands for Cardholder Unique Identifier. See the latest version of NIST SP 800-73 for a complete definition.

4.7   Electronic Cloning

If an attacker has successfully conducted a skimming, sniffing, or social engineering attack, he or she possesses verbatim copies of some of the data objects from an issued PIV Card. The objects that are signed (e.g., the certificates and CHUID) retain their signatures, and the signatures are valid if the original card is valid. The attacks described, however, cannot copy the private or secret keys needed for cryptographic authentication methods. The attacker is thus able to create a partial clone of the PIV Card that would succeed in CHUID-based authentication, but is not able to create a clone that would succeed in PKI or CAK authentication mechanisms.

> *The PIV Card mitigates the risk of electronic cloning by providing the PKI and CAK alternative mechanisms. It is strongly recommended that agencies use PKI or asymmetric CAK challenge/response methods instead of the CHUID authentication mechanism (see the Recommendation in Section 4.9).*

4.8   Electronic Counterfeiting

An attacker could construct a battery-powered, microprocessor-based device that emulates a PIV Card for purposes of the CHUID authentication mechanism. The attacker could program the microprocessor to generate and test CHUIDs repetitively against a PACS reader, changing the FASC-N credential identifier on each trial. This approach would not require prior capture of a valid CHUID, but since the counterfeit CHUIDs would not possess valid issuer signatures, a successful exploit depends on the absence of signature verification in the CHUID processing done by the reader.

> *The PIV Card mitigates the risk of electronic counterfeiting by storing a CHUID with a digital signature field. Electronic counterfeiting will be extremely difficult if CHUID signature verification is done, although signature verification is not required by FIPS 201. Moreover, since many CHUIDs may be presented while an attacker probes for a valid CHUID, the PACS should employ methods to detect, alarm, and block repeated unsuccessful CHUID presentations.*

4.9   Other Threats

The PIV System and PACS are complex, and this brief discussion has focused on properties of the PIV Card. A number of other attack vectors have not been discussed in detail, including sophisticated technical attacks against the integrity of the PIV Card, PIV System, or PACS components, and cryptanalysis of the PIV cryptographic algorithms. While the impact of successful attacks such as these could be moderate to high, the probability of success is believed to be extremely low.

> **Recommendation:** This section emphasizes the technical risks that remain with the CHUID authentication mechanism. If the CHUID authentication mechanism were implemented without restriction, operational risk would increase as the value of targets and the availability of cloning and counterfeiting tools increase. NIST therefore recommends that the CHUID authentication mechanism be implemented in only two situations: 1) access control points separating two areas at the same impact level, either Controlled or Limited; and 2) combined with the VIS authentication mechanism at access points between Unrestricted and Controlled areas. See Section 7 for further detail. NIST further recommends that the asymmetric CAK authentication mechanism be used instead of the CHUID authentication mechanism to the greatest extent practical.

5.   Limitations of Deployed Physical Access Control Systems

FIPS 201 and its supporting special publications impose specific requirements on PACS interfaces with PIV Card and PIV System. These requirements will present technical challenges in migrating to PIV Card use in the areas of cardholder identification, card-to-reader interface, and authentication protocol. The following sections explore how FIPS 201 requirements differ from the capabilities of currently deployed PACS that are not PIV-enabled.

5.1   Cardholder Identification

PACS that are currently deployed in Federal government facilities use cards with data formats that are often proprietary to the specific enterprise. Many of the installed PACS use an ID number based on a 26-bit standard, which is comprised of an 8-bit site code and a 16-bit unique card ID number with 2 bits assigned to parity (the parity bits add confidence that the data transmission has no errors). The 8-bit site code accommodates 256 unique sites and the 16-bit card ID number accommodates 65,536 unique users for that site. Larger ID numbers are used by some systems but they are not necessarily interoperable.

A PACS based on the 26-bit format is deployed as a standalone solution at a dedicated site. Typically, these solutions are managed locally, and an individual with an access card for one site cannot use the same card at a second site and must obtain a second card. FIPS 201 changes this dynamic because the credential is issued through a separate process instead of as part of the PACS deployment. Deployed PACS need to be upgraded or re-provisioned to support at least a 14 decimal digit FASC-N Identifier.

5.2   Door Reader Interface

Deployed PACS readers come in varying configurations and offer multiple interface options for the card and the Controller. FIPS 201 standardizes the use of the ISO/IEC 14443 interface for the contactless reader to card communication. Note that the card reader may require additional conformance testing for Federal acquisition. An authority for such conformance testing is the [FIPS 201 Evaluation Program] which defines tests and maintains a list of approved products. Not all existing PACS use this interface, so some agencies may have to plan to migrate from their existing environment to the ISO/IEC 14443 conformant interface. Alternatively, an agency may use the contact interface based on ISO/IEC 7816.

The interface from the Door Reader to the Controller also comes in different configurations. FIPS 201 does not specify which protocols can be used for this interface, provided the necessary data can be communicated to the Controller. Typical deployed implementations support transmitting a small amount of data (on the order of 10 to 15 bytes), but FIPS 201 defines data elements which are much larger. Therefore, depending on the agency's implementation strategy, an upgrade to the Door Reader to Controller interface may also be required. At a minimum, a 14 decimal digit FASC-N Identifier will be supported in most cases. Note that any change to this interface may also necessitate changes to the physical wiring and cabling infrastructures.

5.3   Authentication Capability

Deployed PACS readers use proximity or magnetic stripe technology to interface with identity cards and use proprietary protocols to communicate data. Some of these proprietary protocols employ cryptography, but their use is limited to the local site. FIPS 201 specifies identity credentials that could be used for a new generation of identity management technology for building access. FIPS 201 and its supporting special publications define the credential data model and the card-to-reader interface, and also provide requirements for implementing the digital certificates.

FIPS 201 added a standardized contactless and contact interface, biometric fingerprint, and cryptography to the credential that could be used to attain a higher level of identity authentication assurance. The capability to perform bi-directional data communication is fundamental to the deployment of secure building access. Adding cryptography to the credentials permits agencies to validate the data objects on the card and authenticate the cardholder. Adding credential expiration and on-line credential validation requirements also strengthens access control decisions. At the same time, FIPS 201 provided the opportunity to migrate building access systems from LITTLE OR NO confidence assurance levels to VERY HIGH confidence assurance levels. Existing PACS may need upgrades to take advantage of these features and functions, in coordination with the following guidelines and authorities:

+ FIPS 201 assurance levels

+ Department of Justice Vulnerability Assessment Report of Federal Facilities

+ OMB M-04-04, E-Authentication Guidance for Federal Agencies. [M-04-04]

FIPS 201 redefines the requirements for building access in a fundamental way: instead of each facility issuing an access card solely for that facility's defined PACS architecture, a facility relies on the PIV Card that was issued by the same, or a different, agency certified by the Federal government. The facility still has control over the user's access privileges, but the technology has been standardized to optimize inter-agency interoperability and the credential has been issued to the user as part of the FIPS 201 identity management process.

5.4   Deployed Wiring

Selecting a particular reader type and its interface with the Controller requires careful attention to wiring. Existing wiring should be assessed for its ability to meet the requirements of new readers and Controllers. The existing wiring may be a limiting factor due to its capacity to transmit data and original specifications. Many recently installed systems use higher bandwidth cables, which are typically sufficient for a PIV-based access control system. In some environments, advanced signaling methods operating at higher speeds with lower signal-to-noise margins can necessitate upgrades to the wiring.

5.5   Software Upgrades

Vendors may be able to upgrade their existing PACS software to minimize the hardware changes needed for an existing PACS to accept PIV Cards. Software or firmware upgrades to Controllers or Door readers may be available to agencies. PACS suppliers should be asked if software or firmware upgrades supporting PIV Cards are a possibility. If available, the agency should ensure that the software upgrade will have no adverse effect on the PACS system or any interconnected systems.

5.6   Deployed Non-PIV PACS Cards and PIV Card Differences

The list below compares the basic differences in the technology offerings between the deployed Non-PIV PACS cards and the PIV Card.

+ Some deployed PACS use site-specific card technology, with the result that a card cannot be used at sites with incompatible PACS. For example, a magnetic stripe card cannot be used at a proximity card site, and a magnetic stripe card from one vendor cannot be used at a site with magnetic stripe equipment from another vendor.

+ Deployed PACS readers can read an identifying number from a card, but in most cases they do not perform a cryptographic challenge/response exchange. Many Non-PIV PACS cards can be copied easily.

+ When two sites use compatible card technology, the risk of duplicate site identifiers for cards is always present. Without government-wide coordination of identifiers, the same identifier could be used on multiple cards at different sites.

+ To achieve government-wide coordination of cardholder identifiers, enough identifiers must be available for all government-issued credentials. Many deployed PACS have a limit on the number of sites (256) and the number of users per site (65,536) that is too small for government-wide use and can lead to the same identifiers being issued to different individuals.

+ Deployed PACS control expiration of credentials through an expiration date stored in a site database, whereas with PIV Cards expiration dates can be obtained from the cards themselves. There is no simple way to synchronize the expiration of credentials for a Federal employee or contractor with access to multiple sites unless all sites are tied into a centralized database for the deployed PACS.

+ Use of PINs, public key infrastructure, and biometrics with deployed PACS is managed on a site-specific basis at the PACS server. Individuals must enroll PINs, keys, or biometrics at each site. Since PINs, keys, and biometrics are often stored in a site database, they may not be technically interoperable with the requirements of other sites.

FIPS 201-conformant PACS eliminate or substantially reduce each of these limitations, relative to deployed PACS installations.

6. The PIV Vision

HSPD-12 begins, "Wide variations in the quality and security of forms of identification used to gain access to secure Federal and other facilities where there is potential for terrorist attacks need to be eliminated." HSPD-12 continues, in Paragraph 2, "As promptly as possible… the heads of executive departments and agencies shall, to the maximum extent practicable, require the use of identification by Federal employees and contractors that meets the Standard in gaining physical access to Federally controlled facilities…"

HSPD-12 directs Federal departments and agencies to improve identification and authentication of Federal employees and contractors requiring access to Federally controlled facilities through the widespread application of FIPS 201. The standard defines the characteristics of the PIV System. This section describes the benefits that are expected from the use of the PIV System, to the maximum extent practicable, for authenticating people to PACS managed by the United States Government.

This section focuses on the benefits of electronic verification and direct integration with an electronic PACS. The VIS authentication mechanism, which must be verified manually, is applicable to physical access control, as described in other sections of this publication. The FIPS 201 authentication mechanisms that can be performed electronically are CHUID, PKI, BIO, and BIO-A. NIST SP 800-73, included by reference in FIPS 201, defines an additional, optional authentication mechanism, CAK. [SP800-73]

6.1 Interoperability

In this publication, the term interoperability means the ability to use any PIV Card with any PACS application performing one or more PIV authentication mechanisms. The data objects and keys placed on a PIV Card during issuance use specific cryptographic algorithms selected from the acceptable algorithms in [SP800-78]. A PACS application can interrogate the card to learn which algorithms are used. To attain full interoperability, a relying PACS application will need to support all acceptable algorithms, key lengths, and key material that could be presented, either by a PIV Card or by the PIV infrastructure.

The interoperability goal of the PIV-enabled PACS can be stated:

1. Any PIV Card can provide proof of identity to any electronic PACS (access is granted only if the identity is so authorized).

2. After a successful authentication, the authentication mechanism provides the cardholder's authenticated identity, in the form of a FASC-N Identifier (a subset of FASC-N as defined in Section 3), to the relying party.

To achieve interoperability, the PACS should at least observe the following conditions:

+ If the PKI authentication mechanism is performed by a PACS application, the PACS should support all of the asymmetric algorithms permitted for the PIV Authentication Key, as specified in Table 3-1 of [SP800-78], i.e., RSA 1024 (through 31 December 2013), RSA 2048, and ECDSA P-256, and the PACS should accept all valid PIV authentication certificates and require PIN entry.

+ If the CAK authentication mechanism is performed by the PACS, the accepted algorithms will be the same, but the PACS will accept only Card Authentication Key certificates and not require PIN entry.

+ If CHUID authentication with signature verification is performed, the PACS should support all of the signature algorithms and key sizes permitted by Table 3-3 of [SP800-78]. If only CHUID authentication without signature verification of the CHUID is performed, no cryptographic operations are performed, and no cryptographic requirement is placed on the PACS.

+ PINs required for PIV authentication mechanisms are strings of eight or fewer decimal digits. For PKI, BIO, and BIO-A authentication mechanisms, a PIN entry device must acquire PINs from the cardholder and present them to the PIV Card to activate the card.

The PIMM presented in Section 9 can be used to measure progress towards the interoperability goal. When PIV implementation is complete, all installed PACS readers will be approved products on the GSA HSPD-12 Evaluation Program Approved Products List, and each will be capable of one or more PIV authentication mechanisms. [FIPS 201 Evaluation Program] At this time, any PIV Card will be able to perform any authentication mechanism it has been issued to perform at any PACS.

The ability of a PIV Card and cardholder to authenticate at a reader does not mean they will be granted access—it means only that the cardholder has been identified, with the assurance level of the authentication mechanism employed, to the reader. A cardholder must authenticate **and be authorized** to be granted access. Authorization policies and mechanisms are outside the scope of FIPS 201.

> **Recommendation:** To obtain the full benefit of PIV interoperability, HSPD-12 project managers should ensure that relying systems have the capability to use all cryptographic algorithms that apply to the authentication mechanism(s) performed. Departments and agencies should procure and deploy HSPD-12 products on the GSA HSPD-12 Evaluation Program Approved Products List where applicable, and can use the PIMM presented in Section 9 to measure progress toward the goal of interoperability. [FIPS 201 Evaluation Program]

6.2 Qualities of the Complete Implementation

The PIV System implementation will be complete when the following qualities have been achieved.

1. PIV authentication mechanisms are used wherever they are applicable, in accordance with HSPD-12 and FIPS 201.

2. Electronic authentication (as opposed to VIS authentication) is the common practice.

3. Electronic validation of the PIV Card is done at or near the time of authentication.

4. All PIV Card access control decisions are made by comparing an initial string of the FASC-N Identifier against the ACL entries. See Appendix B for details and examples.

5. PIV authentication mechanisms are applied based on the impact assessed for the area.

6. Cryptographic and biometric authentications are applied widely in moderate- and high-impact [FIPS199] areas.

7. Agencies exhibit reciprocal trust in the process assurance of PCIs.

8. Both new and upgraded PACS applications accept PIV Cards as proof of identity for user registration/provisioning, user authentication, or both.

HSPD-12 declares its goals are to "…enhance security, increase Government efficiency, reduce identity fraud, and protect personal privacy," and states specific criteria to be met by the implementation:

> "Secure and reliable forms of identification" for purposes of this directive means identification that (a) is issued based on sound criteria for verifying an individual employee's identity; (b) is strongly resistant to identity fraud, tampering, counterfeiting, and terrorist exploitation; (c) can be rapidly authenticated electronically; and (d) is issued only by providers whose reliability has been established by an official accreditation process. The Standard will include graduated criteria, from least secure to most secure, to ensure flexibility in selecting the appropriate level of security for each application."

The Federal Information Security Management Act [FISMA] mandated the standardization of security management practices for information systems. The foundational concept of FISMA security management is impact assessment and impact-based planning ("impact" being a generalization of "exposure" to monetary and non-monetary damage). FIPS 201 follows this methodology by implementing authentication mechanisms at three E-Authentication confidence levels (SOME, HIGH, and VERY HIGH). A gap remains, however, between the concepts of impact and confidence levels. This document suggests a method to close this gap through the use of risk-based planning and the establishment of "Controlled, Limited, Exclusion" boundaries for appropriately protecting facility assets or resources.

Interoperability of PIV Cards and PIV authentication mechanisms is not a guaranteed consequence of the technical standard. Government-wide interoperability also requires Federal agencies to exhibit reciprocal trust in the processes of PCIs and the service quality of the PIV Card validation and revocation infrastructure. Reciprocal trust is enabled by the requirements for the PIV issuance process stated in FIPS 201, and supported by the Accreditation process methodology described in NIST SP 800-79. [SP800-79] Trust is built when the technical standard is thorough, unambiguous, and grounded in practical requirements; when the conformance and audit processes are documented and uniformly practiced; and when positive PIV System audit results are available to the community of relying parties.

> **Recommendation:** Once all appropriate authentication mechanisms are satisfied, access control decisions are made by comparing the 14 decimal digit FASC-N Identifier, and optionally the values of additional FASC-N fields, against the ACL entries.

> **Recommendation:** As agencies develop risk-based implementation plans, they will create and evolve plans for PIV Card issuance and application integration. They might consider which of the eight qualities are most relevant to agency goals and priorities, and derive further project objectives, metrics, and milestones from those qualities. They should also consider the relation of HSPD-12 to FISMA requirements, and examine the potential for cost tradeoffs where PIV can replace more expensive authentication methods.

6.3   Benefits of the Complete Implementation

The complete PIV System will be an identity infrastructure that is attractive to Federal agencies, application owners, and contractors because of these benefits:

+ Enhanced trust. PIV Cards will be issued in accordance with a standardized, audited process, which will exceed the best practice level for low- and moderate-impact applications today, and equal best practice reached for high-impact applications.

+ Resistance to misuse and cloning. Electronic validation of the PIV Card, using digital signatures, makes it tamper-resistant. Cryptographic challenge/response protocols make the PIV Card counterfeit-resistant. Biometric authentication makes the PIV Card non-transferable.

+ Status and revocation. PIV Card Issuer process assurance will extend beyond the issuance action to PIV Card validation and revocation services. These services are required elements of the PIV infrastructure, and will be implemented, monitored, and audited with the same care as the PIV issuance process.

+ Standard identity infrastructure. Application developers will assume, as a default, that registration and authentication will use a PIV Card identity, reducing development cost, registration time, and the application learning curve for new subjects.

+ Integrated system. PACS will be fully integrated with other PIV system components that perform provisioning, enrollment, and finalization.

+ Fewer passwords. A single PIV Card provides a small set of authentication methods that are applicable to many applications and in many contexts. This means significantly fewer passwords and account enrollments.

Each of these points both enhances security and creates efficiency of operation. Reducing passwords and password helpdesk calls, reusing identity enrollment across multiple applications, collapsing redundant status and revocation processes (separate processes for revocation on termination across multiple applications), and replacing authentication credentials that are easily shared or transferred will reduce operating costs borne by Federal agencies. Availability of a skilled workforce familiar with the standardized PIV identity infrastructure, implementation of PIV issuance with a standardized identity verification methodology, the existence of high-availability on-line services for PIV Card status and validation, and pre-enrollment in a graduated, multi-factor authentication scheme all enhance security current practice in many applications. The replacement of password (single-factor) authentication with PIV Card (one, two, or three-factor) authentication is a fundamental advance in authentication assurance.

Biometric enrollment is mandatory for the PIV Card. Every government employee and contractor who can provide at least one fingerprint image of acceptable quality will be pre-enrolled for biometric authentication.[5] In the complete PIV System, the marginal cost for biometric enrollment to the application owner, relative to other authentication mechanisms, is near zero, enabling more applications to gain the benefits of biometric authentication.

> **Recommendation:** Operational metrics should be designed to measure actual benefits over the operational lifetime of the PIV System. They may be derived by formulating each of the expected benefits above as a service quality metric, e.g., for "integrated system", service quality could be defined as the percentage of

---

[5] [FIPS201] Section 4.4.1 states that "In cases where there is difficulty in collecting even a single fingerprint of acceptable quality, the department or agency shall perform authentication using asymmetric cryptography as described in Section 6.2.4." Also, see [SP800-76] Section 3.3 and 3.4.

PACS registrations that are performed automatically by provisioning from the PIV issuance system.

6.4   Infrastructure Requirements

The qualities and benefits of the complete PIV System can only be achieved if its implementation is supported by general advances in infrastructure used by PACS. The following areas have significant influence on the rate at which the complete PIV System integration can be achieved by PACS, and should therefore be supported by PACS upgrades and new PACS procurements:

1. Fast, two-way communication between readers and controllers or panels

2. Fast network communication between readers, controllers, or panels and PIV status and validation services

Point (1) allows readers to access cached validation status during access control transactions. Point (2) allows controllers or panels to cache the validation status. Points (1) and (2) combined could allow readers direct access to PIV status and validation services, if needed.

> **Recommendation**: Maximum benefit will be obtained from the PIV System when it is adequately supported by infrastructure. Infrastructure upgrades may be justified, especially to improve communication among PACS system elements (e.g., support two-way communication).

7.   PIV Authentication Mechanisms

This section provides a discussion of PIV authentication mechanisms and their application in PACS environments. PIV authentication mechanisms offer a range of security measures (of different throughputs) that can be applied in a PACS environment. This section first describes a measurement scale for security relevant to PACS environments. Then it discusses security offerings of each PIV authentication mechanism and their combinatory effects on identity authentication. Finally, this section provides recommendations on the use of PIV authentication mechanisms in a PACS environment.

7.1   Authentication Factors

One of the functions of the PACS application is to verify the identity of the cardholder presenting a PIV Card. The PACS application may perform one or more authentication mechanisms using the PIV Card to establish confidence in the identity of the cardholder. The authentication of an identity is based on the **verification** of one, two, or three of these factors: a) "something you have", for example, possession of the PIV Card; b) "something you know", for example, knowledge of the PIN; and c) "something you are", for example, presentation of live fingerprints by a cardholder.

The PIV Card authentication mechanisms operate in several different ways, as defined in [FIPS201], [SP800-73], and [SP800-76]. For example, a data object may be read from the PIV Card and its signature verified (CHUID authentication mechanism). A private key on the PIV Card may be used to sign a challenge (PKI and CAK authentication mechanisms). A valid biometric may be read from the card and compared against a live fingerprint scan (BIO and BIO-A authentication mechanisms).

Also, PIV Card authentication mechanisms may be performed by different entities, referred to here as verifiers. For example, a PACS application verifies the signature on a data object, or the signing of a challenge using a private key or comparison of biometric templates. The verifier can also be the PIV Card itself. For example, the PIN is verified by the PIV Card. The PIN verification by the PIV Card should be trusted by the PACS only if the card is trusted to be a valid PIV Card. For example, when PKI + BIO(-A) authentication mechanisms are combined, or CAK + BIO(-A) authentication mechanisms are combined, all three factors are achieved. The PIN verification by the card can be trusted by the PACS because the PIV Card has authenticated to the PACS using the PKI or CAK authentication mechanisms, respectively.

The confidence in the cardholder's identity increases with the number of factors used to authenticate the PIV Card. Table 7-1 provides a list of PIV authentication mechanisms and their authentication factors. Note that CAK + BIO(-A) authentication mechanism is recognized as a unique combination in this table. This is due to the fact that neither CAK nor BIO(-A) individually provide "something you know" authentication factor, but when they are used together, PIN verification provides this factor. Many different combinations of the Table 7-1 authentication mechanisms are possible and an exhaustive list of combinations is provided in Appendix C.

Table 7-1. Authentication Factors of PIV Authentication Mechanisms

PIV Authentication Mechanism	Have	Know	Are	Authentication Factors (HKA Vector)	Interface
CAK + BIO (-A)	x	x	x	3	Contact
BIO-A x			x	2	Contact
PKI x		x		2	Contact
BIO			x	1	Contact
CAK x				1	Contact/ Contactless
CHUID + VIS	x			1	Contact/ Contactless

Each of the above PIV authentication mechanisms is described further in the following sections.

7.1.1 Deployed Proximity or Magnetic Stripe Authentication

Deployed proximity and magnetic stripe authentication are not PIV authentication mechanisms and when used in conjunction with PIV authentication mechanisms, there is a strong potential for "collisions". Proximity and magnetic stripe card technology read a number from a card and send it to the Controller. The Controller compares this number against its database to make the access control decision. If a deployed system does not include an agency code in the numbers compared, an out-of-agency cardholder may be mistakenly accepted as an authorized site user. Refer to Appendix B for additional details. Moreover, proximity and magnetic stripe cards can be easily counterfeited or cloned.

7.1.2 Visual (VIS) Authentication

Visual authentication entails inspection of the topographical features on the front and back of the PIV Card. The human guard checks to see that the PIV Card looks genuine, compares the cardholder's facial features with the picture on the card, checks the expiration date printed on the card, verifies the correctness of other data elements printed on the card, and visually verifies the security feature(s) on the card. The effectiveness of this mechanism depends on training, skill, and diligence of the guard (to match the face in spite of changes in beard, mustache, hair coloring, eye glasses, etc.)—counterfeit IDs and banknotes can pass visual inspections easily. Digital scanners, printers, and image editing software have made counterfeiting easier. Moreover, the visual verification of security features does not scale well across agencies since each agency may implement different security features.

7.1.3 Cardholder Unique Identifier (CHUID) Authentication

The CHUID, as defined in FIPS 201, is one of the data objects on PIV credentials. The CHUID includes a FASC-N data element that uniquely identifies the PIV Card. The CHUID also uniquely identifies an individual since each PIV Card is issued to an individual. The CHUID data object is signed by the issuer so alterations or modifications to a CHUID can be detected.

The CHUID is standardized by FIPS 201; therefore, a CHUID data object can be counterfeited easily with the exception of the issuer signature. A counterfeit CHUID would not possess a valid issuer signature. The CHUID is a free read object on the PIV Card; therefore, it can be read or cloned easily. Because of the risk of CHUID counterfeiting or cloning, the CHUID authentication mechanism, used in isolation, provides a confidence level that is comparable to proximity cards in widespread use today. However, if the CHUID signature verification is performed, the PACS can be sure the CHUID came from a valid issuer and it has not been altered. Reading the CHUID from a PIV Card is not sufficient to establish confidence in cardholder's identity. Therefore, in order to achieve single-factor authentication with CHUID, the relying parties must validate the signature on the CHUID.

7.1.4   Card Authentication Key (CAK) Authentication

The CAK is an optional key that may be present on any PIV Card. As the name implies, the purpose of the CAK authentication mechanism is to authenticate the card and therefore its possessor. The CAK is unique among the PIV keys in several respects:

1. The CAK may be used on the contactless or contact interface in a challenge/response protocol;

2. The use of the CAK does not require PIN entry; and

3. NIST strongly recommends that every PIV Card contain an asymmetric CAK and corresponding certificate, and that PACS use an asymmetric challenge/response CAK protocol. However, [FIPS201] permits the CAK on a specific card to be either asymmetric or symmetric.

Points (1) and (2) were intended to allow the CAK to be used for one-factor authentication to PACS readers. The result will still remain a one-factor authentication. CAK authentication mechanism examples are given in [SP800-73], Appendix B.

Point (3), specifically the asymmetric CAK, ensures that government-wide interoperability among PACS applications is preserved. Due to the optionality and algorithm variability of the CAK permitted by [FIPS201], agency specific symmetric CAK authentication will not scale to an interoperable authentication mechanism across agencies. For this reason, NIST recommends that asymmetric CAK be encouraged as the interoperable, single-factor PIV authentication mechanism for PACS.

> **Recommendation:** NIST strongly recommends that every PIV Card contain an asymmetric CAK and corresponding certificate, and that PACS use an asymmetric challenge/response CAK protocol.

7.1.5   PIV Authentication Key (PKI) Authentication

PACS may be designed to perform public key cryptography-based authentication using the PIV Authentication Key. Use of the PKI provides two-factor[6] authentication, since the cardholder must enter a PIN to unlock the card in order to successfully authenticate.

When using the PKI authentication mechanism, FIPS 201 requires the PACS to determine the validity of certificates at the time an individual presents his or her card to a card reader. This may

---

[6] Two-factor authentication is a system wherein two different methods are used to authenticate. An example of two-factor authentication is a verification of "something you have" and "something you know". Using two factors as opposed to one delivers a higher level of authentication assurance.

be done on-line in real-time, or it may be implemented by pre-validating the certificates and caching the results. Section 7.4 specifies procedures for performing public key cryptography-based authentication under the assumption that only individuals who are pre-enrolled will be granted access.[7] Section 7.5 further describes the caching status proxy.

7.1.6 BIO Authentication

PACS may be designed to perform biometric authentication using the fingerprint information stored on the PIV Card.[8] The biometric on the PIV Card is signed by the issuer, so the authenticity of the biometric can be checked by the PACS. Verification of the signature on the biometric data object, and matching of the reference biometric template with the sample biometric template, is performed by the PACS application. The verification of signature and matching of biometric results in one-factor authentication. This authentication mechanism does not include authentication of the PIV Card. Potentially, a biometric template could be placed on a fake card, so neither the "something you have" nor "something you know" factors are validated. As a result, this document rates the BIO authentication mechanism as a one-factor ("something you are") authentication mechanism. BIO combined with cryptographic challenge/response, PKI + BIO or CAK + BIO, authenticates the PIV Card and thus achieves three-factor authentication.

> **Recommendation:** A PACS should *always* verify the digital signature on the biometric template data object, and do path validation, before performing a match. Otherwise, the result of the match should not be trusted.

> **Recommendation:** Biometric readers, especially those used at access points to Limited and Exclusion areas, should have a proven capability to accept live fingers and reject artificial fingers. Biometric readers, especially unattended readers in an Unrestricted area, should be physically hardened to protect against direct electrical compromise.

7.1.7 BIO-A Authentication

This authentication mechanism is the same as BIO authentication but an attendant supervises the use of the PIV Card and the submission of the PIN and the sample biometric by the cardholder. Some fingerprint biometric readers have been shown to accept fake or synthetic fingerprints; others may allow access to internal wiring with relative ease. The presence of an attendant during BIO-A authentication serves to mitigate these risks. Moreover, the presence of an attendant also provides increased assurance, relative to BIO, that a fake card is not being used, which accounts for an additional authentication factor of "something you have." Since the PIN is verified by the PIV Card and the card itself is not verified by PACS, the "something you know" authentication factor is not validated. In summary, the BIO-A authentication mechanism benefits from a presence of visual, but not from a strong challenge/response authentication, with the PIV Card. Therefore, BIO-A is considered a two-factor authentication mechanism.

---

[7] Pre-enrolling a certificate is not the same as pre-authorizing the identity for access. Pre-enrolling means only that a valid identity is known to the PACS. Authorization decisions for known identities are made separately.

[8] There will be instances where a PIV Card does not store two fingerprint templates with an acceptable quality score. In these cases, follow the recommendations stated in FIPS 201 Section 4.4.1, "In cases where there is difficulty in collecting even a single fingerprint of acceptable quality, the department or agency shall perform authentication using asymmetric cryptography as described in Section 6.2.4." and [SP800-76] Sections 3.3 and 3.4. Alternatively, agency security policy may require additional authentication mechanisms in consideration of impact-based security management.

7.1.8 CAK + BIO(-A) Authentication

As discussed in Section 7.1.6 and 7.1.7, BIO(-A) by itself does not provide three-factor authentication. However, when BIO(-A) and CAK authentication mechanisms are performed at the same time, the verification of the PIN can be trusted because the PIV Card is authenticated by CAK. CAK + BIO(-A) is listed in Table 7-1 because the combined authentication mechanism is judged to achieve three-factor authentication (which would not be predicted by the sum of the HKA vectors of CAK + BIO(-A)).[9]

7.2 Multi-Factor Authentication

Possession of a valid PIV Card as evidenced by visual inspection of the card, reading a signed object from the card, or performing challenge/response authentication with the card, provides one-factor authentication. For this reason, the VIS, CHUID, and CAK authentication mechanisms provide one-factor authentication. VIS provides weak one-factor authentication since the card verification is subjective. CHUID also provides weak one-factor authentication since it could be cloned or counterfeited (in absence of signature verification). The BIO mechanism provides one-factor authentication since the reference biometric template is compared against the sample biometric template. The PKI authentication mechanism provides two-factor authentication since it requires possession of the PIV Card and knowledge of the PIN. The BIO-A mechanism provides two-factor authentication since the reference biometric template is compared with the sample biometric template in the presence of an attendant. The BIO-A mechanism requires a PIV Card, knowledge of a PIN, and live fingerprint. The knowledge of a PIN, the third factor of authentication, can only be trusted by combining PKI + BIO(-A) or CAK + BIO(-A) authentication mechanisms. The next section describes the use of multi-factor authentication in the PACS environment.

7.3 Selection of PIV Authentication Mechanisms

A risk-based approach should be used when selecting appropriate PIV authentication mechanisms for physical access to Federal government buildings and facilities. Determining risk to the facility is beyond the scope of this document; however, an agency may use a Facility Security Level (FSL) Determination to derive the FSL for its facilities. There is no simple one-to-one mapping between the FSL and the authentication mechanism(s) that should be employed. An FSL I campus facility may have a need for nested perimeters due to localized high-value assets. An FSL III facility may not have any high-value assets but may be larger in population. An FSL V facility may need the highest level of authentication assurance at all access points except the public entrance to a visitor center.

For these reasons, it is recommended that authentication mechanisms be selected on the basis of protective areas established around assets or resources. This document adopts the concept of "Controlled, Limited, Exclusion" areas as defined in [PHYSEC]. Procedurally, proof of affiliation is often sufficient to gain access to a Controlled area (e.g., an agency's badge to that agency's headquarters' outer perimeter). Access to Limited areas is often based on functional subgroups or roles (e.g., a division badge to that division's building or wing). The individual membership in the group or privilege of the role is established by authentication of the identity of the cardholder. Access to Exclusion areas may be gained by individual authorization only. Federal government facilities can be identified and categorized in these areas and correspond

---

[9] PKI + BIO(-A) also achieves three-factor authentication, but is not present in Table 7-1 because three factors are predicted by the sum of the HKA vectors of PKI and BIO(-A). For all combined mechanisms not in the table, the sum of the HKA vectors correctly predicts the number of factors achieved.

generally to LOW (for Controlled), MODERATE (for Limited), and HIGH (for Exclusion) impact assets or resources [FIPS 199]. This document recommends that Table 7-2 be used to determine the minimum number of authentication factors needed to satisfy security requirements of the area.

Table 7-2. Authentication Factors for Security Areas

Security Areas	Number of Authentication Factors Required
Controlled 1	
Limited 2	
Exclusion 3	

Figure 7-1 illustrates the innermost perimeter at which each PIV authentication mechanism may be used based on the authentication assurance level of the mechanism. Table 7-2 and Figure 7-1 both express constraints on the authentication mechanism that may be selected. The combined effect of Table 7-2 and Figure 7-1 determines exactly what mechanisms may be used. An exhaustive list of possible uses of PIV authentication mechanisms against protected areas is provided in Appendix C.

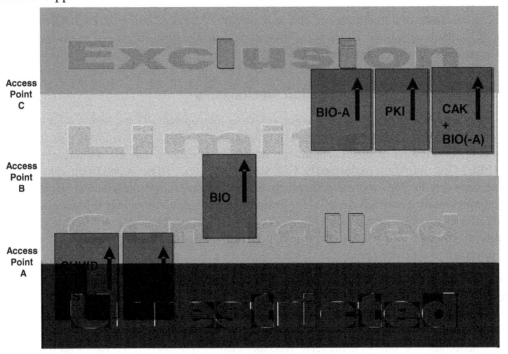

Figure 7-1: Innermost Use of PIV Authentication Mechanisms

The figure should be interpreted with the following notes:

Note 1. "CHUID + VIS" means a combined authentication mechanism performing visual inspection of the PIV Card and CHUID authentication at the same access point. "CAK + BIO(-A)" means a combined authentication mechanism performing CAK and BIO or CAK and BIO-A at the same access point, both using the contact interface of the PIV Card. The term "combine" means that more than one independent authentication mechanisms must successfully authenticate the presenting person, at the same access point, before access is permitted.

Note 2. Authentication mechanisms shown at a perimeter in Figure 7-1 may also be used alone at a perimeter farther out, subject to the requirements in Table 7-2, but not the reverse. If authentication mechanisms are combined in ways not shown in Figure 7-1, at least one of the combined mechanisms must be allowed by Figure 7-1 at the perimeter of use. For example, "BIO and CHUID" could be used at access points A or B, but not at access point C.

Note 3. In a particular facility, a single perimeter may separate areas with a difference of more than one impact level. A single perimeter may allow access from Unrestricted to Limited, Unrestricted to Exclusion, or Controlled to Exclusion areas, and in these cases, the PIV authentication mechanisms should be combined to achieve necessary authentication factors to enter the innermost area.

Note 4. Within a Controlled or Limited area, an access point to an adjacent area at the same impact level may employ any of the authentication mechanisms shown in Figure 7-1, as well as the CHUID authentication mechanism without VIS.

Note 5. Within an Exclusion area, an access point to an adjacent area at the same impact level should use two or three-factor authentication.

Note 6. In most cases, Figure 7-1 and these notes allow flexibility in the selection of specific authentication mechanisms. A decision should be made based on the local security policy and operational considerations.

Note (1) ensures that the CHUID mechanism is combined with VIS where impact level escalation occurs, mitigating the risks described in Section 4.

Notes (3) and (5) ensure that two-factor authentication is always employed to enter Limited areas, and three-factor authentication is employed to enter Exclusion areas. It also ensures that credential validation is done in either case.

Notes (4) and (5) add some flexibility in the case of discretionary access control among areas at the same impact level.

The authentication mechanisms in Figure 7-1 apply at all Threat Condition levels. At Threat Conditions Green, Blue, and Yellow, the facility should use the authentication mechanisms at each perimeter as shown. At Threat Condition Orange, the facility should use two or three-factor authentication at the Controlled perimeters.

When the Threat Condition level increases, some access points may be closed. Access points that remain open should be capable of the required authentication mechanisms at the elevated Threat Condition level.

PIV authentication mechanisms can be mapped to perimeter crossings in many ways, provided that the requirements of this section are met. Figure 7-2 below provides some examples of mapping PIV authentication mechanisms to the perimeter crossings within a facility.

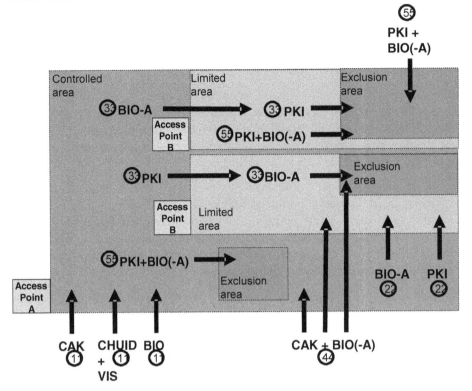

Figure 7-2: Examples of Mapping PIV Authentication Mechanisms

The figure illustrates five different examples. Other sequences of authentication mechanisms are possible. Refer to Appendix C for a complete list of possible combinations of PIV authentication mechanisms that could be used in Federal agency facility environments. Each example below is labeled with a number and is described as follows:

1. CAK, CHUID + VIS, or BIO authentication mechanisms provide one-factor authentication and can be used to cross from Uncontrolled to Controlled areas.

2. BIO-A or PKI authentication mechanisms provide two-factor authentication and can be used to cross into Limited areas. The example shows the BIO-A or PKI authentication mechanism used to cross from Controlled to Limited areas.

3. Authentication in context can be leveraged if the "Controlled, Limited, Exclusion" areas are nested. This example shows that if the BIO or BIO-A authentication mechanism is used to access the Limited area, then the PKI authentication mechanism may be used to control access to the Exclusion area without requiring the cardholder to repeat the BIO or BIO-A authentication mechanism. Conversely, if the PKI authentication mechanism was used to access the Limited area, then BIO-A authentication may be used to control access to the Exclusion area. Authentication in context can be leveraged only when the PACS can store and recall recent access control decision. This in turn would require a cardholder to authenticate at the outer perimeter prior to the inner perimeter. The risk of piggybacking, in which a person follows a cardholder through a door without authenticating, may thus be mitigated by authentication in context.

4. This example shows that an authentication at one level may be used at lower levels. This example shows the CAK + BIO (-A) authentication mechanism may be used to cross from Uncontrolled to Controlled, Uncontrolled to Limited, or Uncontrolled to Exclusion.

5. This example shows that authentication in context is not always possible and a single perimeter may separate areas with a difference of more than one impact level.[10] The example shows that PKI + BIO (-A) authentication mechanism may be used to cross from Uncontrolled to Exclusion, Controlled to Exclusion, or Limited to Exclusion. Note that the three-factor authentication rule is observed in all possible crossings.

Figure 7-2 shows some legitimate examples of mapping PIV authentication mechanisms to the perimeter crossings. There are also authentication mechanisms that do not meet the requirements of Table 7-2. For example, the CAK authentication mechanism should not be used to access Limited or Exclusion areas. Limited and Exclusion require two or three-factor authentication, while CAK only provides one-factor authentication. Also, sometimes combining authentication mechanisms does not add up to the required authentication factors. For example, CAK + PKI is not a valid authentication mechanism to access Exclusion areas. Note that CAK + PKI only provides two factors ("something you have" and "something you know") of authentication.

> **Recommendation:** Authentication assurance will be increased if a PACS uses relevant information from previous access control decisions ("context") when making a new access control decision. For example, if a cardholder attempts to pass from a Controlled to a Limited area, the PACS could require that the cardholder was recently allowed access to the Controlled area. Historically, rigorous implementation of this concept required person-traps and exit tracking, but partial implementations have significant value, and could be strengthened by new technology and systems integration.

7.4   PACS Registration

Before a PACS may grant access to a cardholder, the cardholder must be authorized for access in the PACS. Authorization may be granted to a group of individuals, such as all PIV cardholders, or all PIV cardholders sponsored by a specific agency or bureau (see Appendix B). If authorization is granted to specific individuals, information about the cardholder (specifically, at least the FASC-N) must be added to the PACS Server's authorization database.

If on-line credential validation is performed by the PACS at the time of each authentication (see Section 7.5), the PACS might store no information about the cardholder other than the authorizations and transaction audit log.

If a caching status proxy is employed, information about the cardholder, including the cardholder's certificate, must be added to the server's database. Where one-factor authentication is sufficient, the CAK or PKI certificate may be used. Where at least two-factor authentication is required, the PIV Authentication Key certificate should be used. Enrollment using a caching status proxy should collect and store information required for all FIPS 201 authentication mechanisms needed in the event of increased Threat Condition level.

> **Recommendation:** When a card is terminated, the PIV Card Issuer must revoke all valid authentication certificates for the PIV Card. The authentication certificates include the PIV Authentication Key certificate and the Card Authentication Key certificate (if present).

When the individual is enrolled using a caching status proxy, the enrollment station obtains the PIV Authentication or asymmetric Card Authentication Key certificate from the PIV Card, validates the certificate (including checking the certificate's revocation status), and sends a

---

[10] Although a single perimeter could separate areas with a difference of more than one impact level, this practice may be judged high risk and be prohibited by local security policy.

challenge to the card to verify that the card holds the private key corresponding to the certificate. The authentication certificate is then added to the server's database, along with any other information about the individual that the server maintains (e.g., the individual's authorizations).

Since certificate revocation is used as a mechanism to indicate that a PIV Card should no longer be considered valid, the caching status proxy should periodically re-validate all of the certificates in its database and deactivate the access privileges of any individual whose certificate has expired or has been revoked. Re-validation should be performed by the caching status proxy at least once per day. Once the decision has been made to revoke a PIN credential, agencies may employ local de-authorization methods to supplement revocation and achieve a more rapid local effect.

When an individual presents his or her PIV Card to a door reader, the door reader obtains the authentication certificate from the card, sends a challenge to the card, and then uses the public key in the certificate to verify the response to the challenge.

> **Recommendation:** The CHUID may be collected at registration, but it should be treated as if it were a password (since digital signature provides entropy equivalent to a password) for purposes of retention, i.e., hashed, the hash stored, and the CHUID deleted. A stored CHUID presents risks similar to a stored password; it can be copied and used to gain access. Data elements may be extracted from the CHUID and retained (e.g., the FASC-N, Data Universal Numbering System (DUNS) Number, and Global Unique Identifier (GUID)), and a retained hash is sufficient to enable verification. *NIST strongly recommends against the storage of complete CHUIDs in relying systems.*

> **Recommendation:** PKI and asymmetric CAK authentication mechanisms should be implemented by a PACS reader capable of full certificate path validation, either on-line or using a caching status proxy. Agencies should consider using on-line status checks as a means to reduce the latency of PIV Card status when a PIV Card is used for access to Exclusion areas. If a caching status proxy is used, the certificates should be captured when the PIV Card is registered to the PACS.

7.5   Credential Validation and Path Validation

Credential validation is the process of determining if a presented identity credential is valid, i.e., was legitimately issued and has not expired or been terminated. On-line credential validation is extremely valuable to relying parties because it retrieves the most up-to-date credential status, and can block fraudulent use of a PIV Card that has been terminated as lost or stolen. Credential validation is required by the PKI authentication mechanism, and can be implemented for BIO, BIO-A, CAK, and CHUID authentication mechanisms.

FIPS 201 Section 5.4.5 states, "The presence of a valid, unexpired, and unrevoked PIV authentication certificate on a card is proof that the card was issued and is not revoked." FIPS 201 Section 6.2 further says, "The status of the PIV authentication certificate is directly tied to the status of all other credential elements held by the card." These statements imply that PIV credential validation may be done by performing path validation (see below) on the PIV Authentication Key certificate or Card Authentication Key certificate.

Since the expiration date of a PIV Card is contained in the CHUID, a relying party can determine if a PIV Card has expired by reading the CHUID, verifying the CHUID's signature, then extracting and comparing the expiration date with the current date received from a trusted source.

On-line, on-demand credential validation may not always be practical, due to absence of network connectivity to the PCI, or inadequate response time. In these circumstances, it may be possible for PIV Cards of interest to be registered with a caching status proxy. The caching status proxy can poll the status of all registered cards periodically, and cache the status responses from their issuer(s). Relying parties will see quick query-response service from the caching status proxy. The cache status should be updated at least once every 24 hours.

> **Recommendation:** On-line credential validation should be implemented for all of the FIPS 201 authentication mechanisms whenever possible. It is especially important when the one-factor, non-biometric mechanisms (CHUID, CAK) are used, because they could be exploited by simple possession of a misappropriated PIV Card. Caching techniques can be used to implement credential validation when on-line, on-demand credential validation is not possible. It is also recommended that the cached data be protected against tampering.

Data objects read from a smart card by a reader should not be fully trusted as authentic (i.e., produced by a PCI) and unmodified until their digital signatures are verified. Most data objects in a PIV card-application have embedded digital signatures (i.e., all certificates, the CHUID, fingerprint template, facial image, and security object). The Printed Information Buffer must be signed by the Security Object, and the Card Capability Container may be signed by the Security Object.

Path validation (or *trust path validation*) is the process of verifying the binding between the subject identifier and subject public key in a certificate, based on the public key of a trust anchor, through the validation of a chain of certificates that begins with a certificate issued by the trust anchor and ends with the target certificate. The public key of a trust anchor is implicitly trusted by the relying party (generally, this means it was installed into the relying system by means of a trusted process, such as a direct device-to-device copy). Full trust in a PIV authentication mechanism requires that path validation succeed for each PIV data object used by the mechanism. [11]

The PKI authentication mechanism requires path validation to be performed on the PIV Authentication Key certificate. FIPS 201 does not require that path validation be performed for the BIO, BIO-A, CHUID, and CAK authentication mechanisms; however, these authentication mechanisms can be fully trusted only if path validation is performed. In the absence of path validation, an impostor could forge a fingerprint template and a CHUID object, for example, with signatures from a phony Certification Authority. BIO authentication would succeed with this counterfeit PIV Card, and the forgery would not be detected.

Because credential validation is a special case of path validation, both services can be economically implemented by a single PACS service component.

> **Recommendation:** Path validation should be performed on all signed data objects required by the authentication mechanism in use. Path validation should employ on-line credential validation where possible, or cached certificate status where on-line certificate validation is not possible.

7.6   Lost PIV Card or Suspicion of Fraudulent Use

If a lost PIV Card is found by a person other than the cardholder, or if a pattern of PIV Card activity raises suspicions of fraudulent use, the security office of the issuing agency, or of the cardholder's duty station, should be notified. The security office (issuing and local duty station) will determine if further investigation is warranted and if the PCI should be asked to terminate the

---

[11] If a data object is not used in the authentication mechanism being performed, path validation need not be performed on the data object's digital signature for the authentication result to be fully trusted.

PIV Card. In the event of PIV Card termination, the PCI will request the Certification Authority to revoke certificates on the PIV Card.

8.   PACS Use Cases

HSPD-12 requires that PIV credentials include graduated criteria, from least secure to most secure, for authentication to ensure flexibility in selecting the appropriate level of security for each application. PIV credentials, as defined in FIPS 201, offer a range of security which is discussed in Section 7. This section provides recommendations for the appropriate use of graduated security in PIV credentials for the PACS.

PIV credentials can be used at Federally-owned buildings or leased spaces, single or multi-tenant occupancy, commercial spaces shared with non-government tenants, and government-owned contractor-operated facilities. This includes existing and new construction or major modernizations, standalone facilities, and Federal campuses. Thus, PIV credentials apply to facilities requiring varying levels of security with differing security requirements.

To begin, the agency must know the security requirements for its facility. Since this is beyond the scope of this document, it is assumed that the agency has completed its facility security risk assessment. It is also assumed that the agency is using the FSL Determination[12] to derive the security requirement for its facility. The FSL takes into account size and population, as well as several other factors that capture the value of the facility to the government and to potential adversaries. Other factors, including mission criticality, symbolism, and threat to tenant agency, are also considered. For the purposes of protecting assets and placement of proper security measures, size and population may not be as important as the mission criticality, symbolism, and threat to the tenant agency. Although there is no simple one-to-one mapping between FSL and the authentication mechanism(s), the FSL indicates the general risk to the facility. Based on the FSL, an agency should identify and categorize PACS perimeters as protecting Controlled, Limited, or Exclusion areas. Appropriate security measures can then be implemented based on the areas identified for the facility in consultation with the real property authority and legal authority. This section provides example use cases of PIV authentication mechanisms in the following facility environments:

+ Single-Tenant Facility—A facility that only includes a Federal tenant, or multiple components of the same department or agency that fall under one "umbrella" for security purposes.

+ Multi-Tenant Facility—A facility that includes tenants from multiple Federal departments and agencies, but no non-Federal tenants.

+ Mixed-Multi-Tenant Facility—A facility that includes tenants from multiple Federal departments and agencies as well as one or more non-Federal tenants.

+ Single-Tenant Campus—Federal facilities with two or more buildings surrounded (and thus defined) by a perimeter.

+ Multi-Tenant Campus—Two or more Federal facilities located contiguous to one another and typically sharing some aspects of the environment, such as parking, courtyards, private vehicle access roads or gates, entrances to connected facilities, etc. May also be referred to as a "Federal center" or "Complex".

---

[12] FSL determination is the criteria and process used in determining the facilities security level of a Federal facility.

8.1   Single-Tenant Facility

In single-tenant facilities, a single tenant defines its own security requirements and controls its own security measures. Implementation of security measures is uniform. The facility may be an owned or a leased space. If the space is leased, the tenant usually can impose security requirements based on its needs. This type of facility may range from FSL I to FSL V. Therefore, it may have LOW, MODERATE, or HIGH value assets to protect. Facilities evaluated at FSL I or II may not implement PACS and may continue without PACS. Facilities evaluated at FSL III or above should implement PACS. These facilities may have general access areas where individual identification and authentication is not possible, or necessary. In this case, the agency should establish at least one perimeter beyond which individual authentication is required and conducted with PACS. Figure 8-1 is an example of a Single-Tenant facility. The figure shows a building with multiple floors occupied by one tenant. The one security perimeter is the Lobby where the cardholder authentication takes place. This one-perimeter facility should be designated as a Controlled, Limited, or Exclusion area and the appropriate authentication mechanisms should be selected from Figure 7-1.

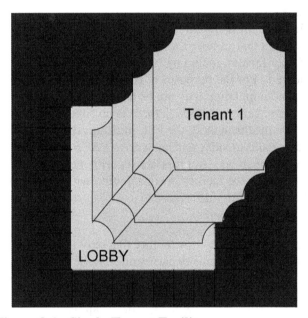

Figure 8-1: Single-Tenant Facility

8.2   Multi-Tenant Facility

The challenge with a multi-tenant facility is to meet the security policies and requirements of the individual tenants in the facility. Some tenants may need higher security than others. The security policies may not be uniform and cannot be imposed upon others. In this situation, a collective (also known as the Building Security Committee) determination has to be made by the designated officials (representatives for each Federal tenant), the owning or leasing department or agency, and the security organization responsible for the facility to identify appropriate areas within the facility. In the end, the decision may be to implement the highest necessary security for the entire facility or to apply the lowest security to the facility while affording individual agencies additional security.

If the highest security is implemented for the entire facility, there is one security perimeter and the security posture is no different from a single-tenant facility. Otherwise, the multi-tenant facility may be viewed as an outer and inner perimeter where different security can be implemented. The outer perimeter is the most common security measure that all the tenants agreed to and the inner perimeter is an agency-specific security measure. For example, the facility may designate Controlled area at the outer perimeter but one of the tenant agencies may require Exclusion area protection. Access to the building may be generally satisfied with a Controlled area authentication mechanism, but the individual agency should implement an Exclusion area authentication mechanism for access to its floor(s). In this example, the building is the outer perimeter while access to an individual floor is the inner perimeter.

Since there are multiple tenants in the facility, it is strongly recommended that each individual tenant designate its own "Controlled, Limited, Exclusion" areas and employ appropriate FIPS 201 authentication mechanisms as in Figure 7-1. Since by definition the multi-tenant facility hosts Federal government employees and contractors, the outer perimeter can be PIV-enabled and individual agencies may piggyback on the authentication performed at the outer perimeter. Figure 8-2 is an example of a multi-tenant facility. The building lobby is the outer perimeter implementing PIV-enabled PACS, while the individual tenants implement additional security perimeters for stronger cardholder authentication.

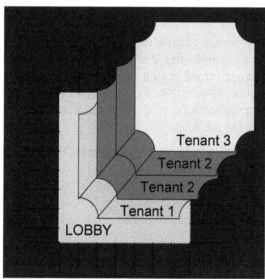

Figure 8-2: Multi-Tenant Facility

8.3 Mixed-Multi-Tenant Facility

The mixed-multi-tenant facility use case is an example of a facility with a mix of PIV cardholders and non-PIV cardholders. Therefore, some tenants in this facility may not possess PIV Cards for authentication. It may be difficult if not impossible to develop one acceptable security policy for all the tenants. The Federal tenants in this facility should ensure they have leverage to implement necessary PIV authentication mechanisms for access to their space. The tenant agencies should designate their own "Controlled, Limited, Exclusion" areas and then evaluate if the facility's PACS will accommodate their security needs. Each Federal government tenant should ensure an appropriate PIV authentication mechanism from Table 7-1 is implemented for its designated areas. If the facility's PACS cannot accommodate agencies' security needs, the tenant agencies should establish their own PACS. This may be considered an inner perimeter to the facility. In this case, the outer perimeter (i.e., access to the building) does not provide any authentication context. The individual agency should manage its own PACS server and user access. In many cases, the tenant agency will not have the authority to implement security measures independently; however, relationships in place should be used to negotiate security measures.

In the event that it is not possible to establish individual PACS and the facility is evaluated at FSL III or above, the tenant should consider the risk involved with inadequate security and make future plans to improve security posture in accordance with the PIMM model in Section 9.

8.4   Single-Tenant Campus

As opposed to a single-tenant facility, a campus is a collection of buildings, labs, and parking spaces that are geographically co-located within a large perimeter. The large perimeter is typically a fenced compound with a gate through which Federal employees, contractors, and visitors gain access. This type of a facility may be assessed at FSL III or above simply due to its population and size. All the areas within the campus may not have the same security requirements. Some spaces may be generally accessible to campus visitors, while some may be specialized spaces such as a high-security lab or a chemical storage area that require a higher level of security protection. In this scenario, one security measure for all spaces might be overbearing and hamper business processes. The campus environment can be further characterized as one big perimeter (outer perimeter) and multiple smaller (inner) perimeters. There are interdependencies between these perimeters that are further elaborated through the "Controlled, Limited, Exclusion" areas.

In the campus environment, a cumulative effect of authentication is achieved as an individual traverses boundaries from unrestricted to Controlled to Limited to Exclusion areas. In other words, authentication performed to gain access to a Controlled area should not be repeated to gain access to a Limited area. Instead, a complementary evidence of identity should be used to achieve multi-factor authentication of the individual who requests access to the Limited area. The same logic applies to the Exclusion area.

Spaces within a campus may have varying degrees of security. The campus may be subdivided into "Controlled, Limited, Exclusion" areas. Moreover, a campus may have one or more areas that are subdivided. A single Controlled or Limited area may be divided into sub-areas for purposes of discretionary or Need-To-Know access control. As a matter of local policy, the use of single-factor authentication may be sufficient to access sub-areas within the same Controlled or Limited area.

The following sections discuss the use of PIV authentication mechanisms in a campus environment with multiple perimeters. This document does not address non-PIV authentication mechanisms.

8.4.1   FSL I or II Campus Facility

Figure 8-3 depicts a security posture of a FSL I or II Campus Facility. It includes one or more Controlled areas that are available to authorized personnel. Since a FSL I or II Campus Facility can be considered a low-risk area, a PACS may or may not be maintained to preclude unauthorized entries. When PACS is maintained, SOME confidence in the identity of the cardholder should be achieved. Implementation of PIV authentication mechanisms for Controlled areas would be an appropriate countermeasure for security at this facility. CHUID + VIS, CAK, or BIO are the three recommended authentication mechanisms in this environment. Note that these authentication mechanisms validate "something you have" or "something you are" (one-factor authentication).

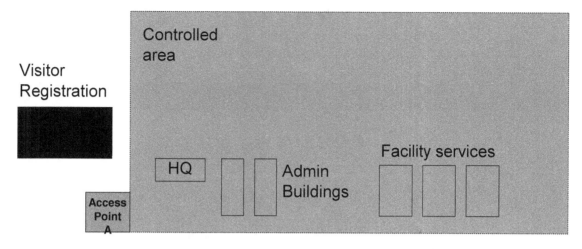

Figure 8-3: FSL II Campus Facility

8.4.2 FSL III Campus Facility

Figure 8-4 depicts a security posture of a FSL III Campus Facility. It includes one or more Controlled areas as well as Limited areas that are restricted to specific group of individuals. Since a FSL III Campus Facility can be considered a moderate-risk facility, a PACS should provide additional security to the more valuable assets. HIGH confidence in the identity of the cardholder should be achieved for access to the Limited area. Note that the entire facility does not need the highest level of security. Access to the Limited area should be complemented with the authentication already completed at the Controlled area. Implementation of BIO-A or PKI authentication mechanisms would be an appropriate countermeasure for the Limited area. Note that these authentication mechanisms validate "something you are" or "something you know" (another factor in authentication).

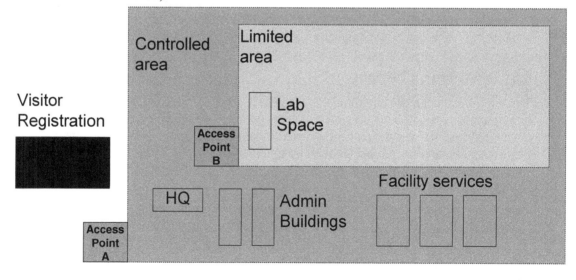

Figure 8-4: FSL III Campus Facility

8.4.3   FSL IV or V Campus Facility

Figure 8-5 depicts a security posture of a FSL IV or V Campus Facility. It includes one or more Controlled areas, Limited areas, and Exclusion areas that are restricted to specific groups of individuals.

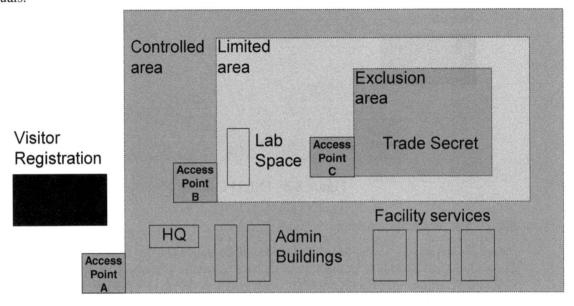

Figure 8-5: FSL IV or V Campus Facility

Although there is not a simple one-to-one mapping between FSLs and PACS Identity Authentication Assurance Levels at access control points, generally higher-risk areas will need stronger identity assurance. Since a FSL IV or V facility is considered a high-risk area, a PACS should achieve VERY HIGH confidence in the identity of the cardholder for access to the Exclusion areas. Note that the entire facility does not need the highest level of confidence in the identity of the cardholder. For access to the Exclusion areas, three-factor authentication should be achieved. This can be accomplished in multiple ways, as shown in Figure 7-2.

8.5   Multi-Tenant Campus

The multi-tenant campus environment is similar to the single-tenant campus except that individual tenants will have their own security policies and the enforcement may be different. A tenant may benefit from the authentication mechanism(s) implemented at the outer perimeter; however, agencies may implement their own PACS within their space. In this case, if an agency were to benefit from other agencies' PACS, its PACS should have communication links with other PACS on the campus.

Once again, each individual tenant within a campus should designate its own "Controlled, Limited, Exclusion" areas and identify appropriate PIV authentication mechanism(s) required for access to its space (see Figure 7-1). The tenants can then determine if they can simply use the campus PACS application, if they should add security by implementing an additional PIV authentication mechanism, or if they should implement a stand-alone PACS. Each individual tenant should ensure that appropriate PIV authentication mechanism(s) from Figure 7-1 are implemented for its designated areas.

8.6 Role-Based Access Control

Authorization of identities enrolled in a PACS is viewed as separate from cardholder authentication. PACS may grant access only to cardholders who were enrolled and authorized in the PACS Server prior to presenting their credentials for authentication, or they may make on-the-fly access control decisions by evaluating the information on presented PIV Cards against a set of access control rules. Because PIV Cards contain only a few mandatory subject attributes (just the Agency Code, Employee Affiliation, and Investigation Status Indicator) that may be used for role-based access control, role or group permissions will usually be derived from off-card information. In the future, standardized role information may be available on-card, especially for Emergency Response Officials or Continuity of Operations (COOP) procedures.

> **Recommendation:** Because having on-card role and permission information would raise difficult challenges concerning update and revocation, PACS permissions should generally be stored in a PACS facilities-based component, such as a panel or controller database.

8.7 Temporary Badges

HSPD-12 mandated the issuance of electronic identity credentials to Federal employees and contractors. OMB Memorandum M-05-24 clarified the eligibility requirements for PIV Cards to temporary Federal employees and contractors, by requiring PIV Card issuance to all Federal employees and contractors who require access to Federal facilities or information systems for more than six months. [M-05-24] Agencies are permitted to issue non-PIV Cards to individuals with access of less than six months. Ineligible personnel (i.e., visitors who are neither Federal employees nor contractors), temporary personnel requiring access for less than six months, eligible personnel who, as a matter of agency policy, are not issued PIV Cards, and PIV cardholders who have forgotten their cards comprise the people who could receive temporary badges. Temporary badges will thus be necessary (although in smaller numbers than before) for the indefinite future.

An agency or facility should consider the relationship of temporary badges to PIV Cards and their PACS system(s) when selecting temporary badge products. Factors to consider during the procurement process include:

+ The OMB M-05-24 requirement that temporary badges be visually and electronically distinguishable from PIV Cards. [M-05-24]

+ Capabilities and costs of enrollment stations, which will likely be local to the facility for best turnaround time.

+ The interoperability of temporary badges with HSPD-12 readers and authentication mechanisms (especially CHUID and CAK for physical access).

+ The assignment of FASC-N unique identifiers to temporary badges, to foster interoperability with HSPD-12 readers.

+ The suitability of contactless-only temporary badges for physical access.

+ The performance, cost, and security tradeoffs between disposable and reusable temporary badges.

+ The importance of VIS authentication mechanisms with temporary badges.

Many approaches to temporary badges are possible. A two-tier approach could become commonplace. A paper-based tier would provide disposable paper badges, with or without printed ID photos. A smart-card tier would issue a reusable card with greater functionality, possibly using PIV Card stock, with capability for physical access, interoperability with HSPD-12 readers and use cases, for periods of weeks to six months.

8.8   Disaster Response and Recovery Incidents

In addition to the use of a PIV credential for cardholder authentication during routine everyday use, the PIV credentials may also be used for access to Federal facilities and Federally controlled areas internal to disaster response and recovery incident scenes. Federal agencies should consider access for personnel from agencies with responsibilities under the National Response Framework, National Incident Management System, National Infrastructure Protection Plan, and the National Continuity Policy Implementation Plan when identifying and categorizing PACS perimeters as protecting Controlled, Limited, and Exclusion areas. Subsequently, agencies should apply appropriate (in accordance with Table 7-2) PIV authentication mechanisms to the areas to ensure that incident management personnel, emergency response providers, and other personnel (including temporary personnel) and resources likely needed to respond to a natural disaster, act of terrorism, or other manmade disaster can be electronically authenticated in order to attain movement internal to Federally controlled facilities and areas within the incident scene.

9.   Migration Strategy

Earlier sections provide the tools agencies will need to prepare a migration plan for PIV enabling their PACS environment. This section discusses how these tools may be used to aid agencies with developing a migration plan.

9.1   Project Planning

Planning for a migration to PIV-enabled PACS should be viewed as an opportunity to modernize deployed PACS. Given the threat environment, as described in Section 4, migrating to PIV-enabled PACS enhances security, fosters trust among agencies, and creates cost efficiencies. This section provides a strategy for developing migration plans, as shown in Figure 9-1.

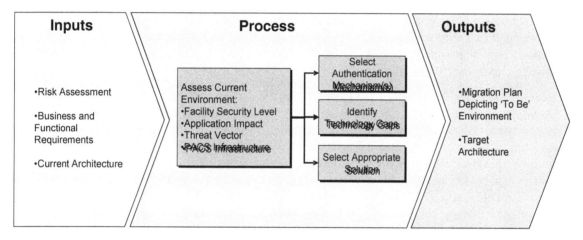

Figure 9-1: Migration Strategy

Planning should be risk-based. Not all access points will require the same level of authentication assurance. Therefore, it is important to start with the risk assessment, which distills into PACS requirements. A migration plan can then be developed to help the agency transition to the desired PIV-enabled PACS environment.

9.2   Risk Assessment

Vulnerability analyses and risk assessments provide a method of prioritizing the criticality of assets (or the impact of the loss of assets), threats, and countermeasure strategies. A structured process allows for the documentation of risks by subject matter experts based on their judgments and assumptions. The final product is a broad set of priorities, both physical and cyber, that contribute to the protection of the critical systems or functions.

The input to this assessment is the understanding of risks in the current environment. Specifically, knowledge of existing vulnerabilities and the impact of attacks should be attained. Section 4 provides attack vectors that must be well-understood and acted upon. The goal should be to embed the countermeasures against the identified threats in migration to PIV-enabled PACS. HSPD-12 requires the standard to provide graduated levels of security in PIV credentials. Note that the combination of one or more authentication mechanisms must be employed to mitigate the counterfeiting, skimming, sniffing, social engineering, and cloning threats.

9.3 Business and Functional Requirements

Each agency has a unique operational environment. Agencies vary in size, organizational structure, and geographic topography. Moreover, their PACS requirements are driven by their mission and by risk and vulnerability assessment. The result is today's PACS environment, which is site-specific and hardly interoperable with other agency implementations. HSPD-12 adds two requirements to these implementations, namely enhanced security and government-wide use of common identification. In other words, an identity credential issued by agency A must be usable by agency B. Note that HSPD-12 leaves the authorization decision to individual agencies. Section 6 provides characteristics of a future PIV-enabled PACS system that substantiates the goals of HSPD-12. Agencies are encouraged to use these characteristics to determine business and functional requirements applicable to their environment.

9.4 Develop Migration Plan

Developing a migration plan requires a vision for PIV-enabled PACS operations. Specifically, a new business process needs to be charted to address the use of PIV credentials. This business process will be dependent on the flexibility available in changing the current environment. Some agencies may be renting spaces where access control is managed by someone else. In the end, however, an agency should have a plan to use the PIV Card.

The OMB Circular Number A-11, Part 7, Section 300: *Planning, Budgeting, Acquisitions, and Management of Capital Assets* establishes policy for the planning, budgeting, acquisition, and management of Federal capital assets, and provides introduction on budget justification and reporting requirements for major IT investments for Federal agencies. OMB Circular A-11 spells out the requirements for supporting several legislative directives including, but not limited to, the Clinger-Cohen Act of 1996, which requires agencies to use a disciplined capital planning and investment control (CPIC) process to acquire, use, maintain and dispose of information technology. In particular, the Clinger-Cohen Act (CCA) specifically instructs the head of each executive agency to establish effective and efficient capital planning processes for selecting, managing, and evaluating the results of all of its major investments in information systems.

In migration planning, agencies should first determine the level of identity assurance required to gain access to their resources. Guidelines on determining the level of identity assurance and selecting a corresponding authentication mechanism are provided in Section 7 of this document. Once authentication mechanisms are selected, agencies will need to identify technology gaps in the existing system. The gaps may be in the existing readers, control panels, or PACS servers. Section 8 discusses prominent scenarios and provides recommendations on filling technology gaps.

It is recommended that agencies plan to ultimately reach the highest level of authentication assurance that displays all the qualities identified in Section 6.2. For this, guidance is provided in the following section to enable agencies to progress in stages.

9.5 Migration Strategy & Tactics

Continuity of operations planning is essential to the success of a migration from deployed PACS to PIV-enabled PACS. Planning lays the strategic framework that makes tactical, moment-to-moment change management possible without catastrophic disruptions. This section suggests sample strategies that can help the tactics succeed.

1. Encourage the project staff to train themselves. In parallel with project planning, create opportunities for the project staff to learn by doing on a small scale.

2. Budget the project carefully. The total cost of ownership (TCO) of a complete PIV-enabled PACS system may be less than the TCO of an upgraded system.

3. In order for any PIV implementation to be successful, cross-departmental collaboration is imperative. The needs of operational units left out of the process may not be fully understood.

4. Look for project synergies. For example, PACS modernization may contribute to facility monitoring, and emergency access policies for First Responders may trigger reevaluation of PACS role models and authentication methods.

5. Develop a relationship with a senior partner. A "senior partner" should be farther along in implementation, or have deeper expertise, than your organization.

6. Consider acquiring access system components that are software and hardware upgradeable to meet anticipated future requirements. For example, an agency may not see the need for contact interfaces at this time; however, it should look to purchase products that either have a dual-interface (contact and contactless capability) or plug-in for contact card readers. The agency may have a choice to add contact readers without replacing the reader infrastructure.

7. Use the extra bandwidth to support remote monitoring and diagnosis, off-loading of service elements, credential validation, cryptographic key management, and so on.

8. Initially, buy multifunction readers that read both deployed and PIV Cards and can perform all PIV electronic use cases—they can be used anywhere. Care should be taken to avoid identifier collisions between two technologies. The agency should design to the highest authentication assurance level that it thinks it may require in the future. Multifunction readers can also implement the authentication mechanism agility required by changing Threat Conditions.

9. As experience and the number of deployed readers grow, select more restricted and cost-effective readers implementing just the required authentication mechanisms.

10. Avoid long-term, side-by-side operation of deployed and PIV technologies. Once PIV Cards have been issued to half the users, cut costs by aggressive completion of the migration.

9.6   PIV Implementation Maturity Model (PIMM)

In a document focused on the integration of PIV authentication mechanisms with PACS systems, it is impossible to provide detailed recommendations on project planning for PACS modifications or upgrades. The planning space is simply too large, due to the variations in local requirements, the asset inventory and impact assessment, project size, the installed base of electronic PACS systems, requirements for integration with other facilities' infrastructure subsystems, etc.

Instead, we recommend in this section a PIMM that can be used to measure the progress of a facility or an agency towards a complete PIV implementation. The PIMM should be applied only to facilities that have established a requirement for an electronic PACS.

The PIMM is organized around the assumption of three enclosing perimeters: the Controlled area, the Limited area, and the Exclusion area, shown in Figure 7-1. In a general sense, "Controlled, Limited, Exclusion" areas may be considered as the security perimeters consistent with protection of low, moderate, and high impact assets, respectively. The following PIMM maturity levels begin by achieving some capability and experience with PIV-based PACS:

1. Maturity Level 1—Ad Hoc PIV Verification. A site has the ability to authenticate PIV Cards by performing required authentication mechanisms on an ad hoc, on-demand basis. For example, card and cardholder authentication is achieved with a handheld terminal or a specific personal computer (PC), for special or occasional uses.

2. Maturity Level 2—Systematic PIV Verification to Controlled Area. At the outer perimeter of the site (Controlled area), PIV Cards are accepted as proof of identity, possibly in addition to currently deployed non-PIV PACS cards. A visitor registration procedure exists to accept PIV Cards and if necessary convert PIV authentication to a currently deployed non-PIV PACS card.

3. Maturity Level 3—Access to Exclusion Areas by PIV or Exception Only. Access to Exclusion areas (the most sensitive areas) is permitted by PIV authentication or "exception" only. Here, exceptions are the exceptions to PIV issuance (e.g., less than six months association). However, all access to exclusion areas is also subject to authorization, and authorization would typically only be granted to PIV cardholders. The exception case might be applied to exclusion areas for Very Important Person (VIP) visitors, for example. At Level 3, currently deployed non-PIV PACS cards are not acceptable for authentication to exclusion areas.

4. Maturity Level 4—Access to Exclusion and Limited Areas by PIV or Exception Only. Access to Limited areas (generally, those permitting clearance level- or role-based authorization) is permitted by PIV authentication or exception only. At Level 4, currently deployed non-PIV PACS cards are not acceptable for authentication to Exclusion or Limited areas. BIO, BIO-A, or PKI are acceptable authentication mechanisms in Limited Areas for authorized PIV cardholders.

5. Maturity Level 5—Access to Exclusion, Limited, or Controlled Areas by PIV or Exception Only. Access to Controlled areas (showing evidence of organizational affiliation, or registration for a visitor, with or without escort) is permitted by PIV authentication or exception only. At Level 5, currently deployed non-PIV PACS cards are not acceptable for authentication to any areas. That is, only the PIV Card is an acceptable credential for Federal employees and contractors.

The first two recommended maturity levels achieve some capability and experience with PIV authentication mechanisms. This capability may exist in parallel with deployed PACS, and after Level 2, the facility has achieved a capability to accept PIV Cards from visitors for access to Controlled areas. The next three maturity levels displace deployed PACS to Exclusion, Limited, and Controlled areas, beginning with the highest-impact areas (with, presumably, the smallest number of access control points and authorized subjects) and moving to the Controlled area (with the largest number of access control points and authorized subjects). At Level 5, the entire facility has been converted to PIV authentication mechanisms at all access points, and/or all subjects, where it is required and appropriate[13].

Maturity levels are progressive: for example, achieving Level 2 requires satisfying all of the requirements of Level 1 in addition to the requirements of Level 2. Maturity levels can be

---

[13] Note that some use of methods other than FIPS 201 authentication mechanisms will continue because not everyone is eligible or required to have a PIV Card.

applied to individual facilities, or by extension to multiple facilities within a bureau or agency. When applied to multiple facilities, a maturity level is achieved when each of the facilities in the group has achieved the maturity level individually.

9.7   PIV-in-PACS Best Practices

HSPD-12 mandates the establishment of government wide identity credentials and the use of these credentials in gaining physical access to Federally controlled facilities. This implies that a PACS application installed at these facilities should interoperate with the credential standardized by [FIPS201], the PIV Card, issued by any government agency. The PIV Card interface and data model requirements are fully specified through [FIPS201] and companion documents. For the PACS application (or PIV-enabled PACS application), the following best practices are recommended.

+   PACS application providers should only employ products that are approved through the FIPS 201 evaluation program where the evaluation program product categories are applicable. [FIPS 201 Evaluation Program]

+   For each access transaction, once the applicable authentication mechanisms are satisfied, all PACS access decisions are based on utilization of the complete FASC-N Identifier (match of the 14 digit Agency Code, System Code, and Credential Number) which is unique across Federal government agencies.

+   The PACS application that uses PKI or asymmetric CAK authentication mechanisms should support all of the asymmetric algorithms specified in Table 3-1 of [SP800-78].

+   Each facility should be mapped to the "Controlled, Limited, Exclusion" model and an assignment of PIV authentication mechanisms to all access control points in accordance with Section 7.1.

+   Signature verification and path validation should be performed on all signed data objects in the PIV authentication mechanisms used.

+   On-line credential validation should be implemented for all authentication mechanisms whenever connectivity is available. Caching techniques may be used to reduce connectivity requirements.

+   The CHUID authentication mechanism should be implemented in only two situations: 1) access control points separating two areas at the same impact level, either Controlled or Limited; and 2) combined with the VIS authentication mechanism at access points between Unrestricted and Controlled areas. See Section 4.9.

+   The CHUID data object may be read from the PIV Card and used for registration and authentication transactions, but should not be retained in a PACS or other relying system after the transaction is complete. If the values of the CHUID data fields must be retained, the asymmetric signature of the CHUID should be deleted.

+   All PACS applications should operate at PIMM Level 5.

10. Future Topics

This section describes advances in FIPS 201 and its associated document suite, and in the architecture and implementation of the PIV infrastructure, that are recommended to realize the full potential of the authentication mechanisms used by PACS.

10.1 Generalized Credential Identifier

FIPS 201 states that the CHUID data object contains the FASC-N data element, "which uniquely identifies each card." The FASC-N actually serves two purposes: 1) identifying a PIV Card (and by correspondence, the cardholder); and 2) binding PIV data objects to the same PIV Card, because the identical FASC-N is contained in the CHUID, the PIV Authentication Key certificate, the Card Authentication Key certificate, the fingerprint biometric record, and the facial image object.

Within the FASC-N, the fundamental card identifier is the (Agency Code, System Code, and Credential Number) triplet called the FASC-N Identifier. Uniqueness of the triplet is derived from a hierarchical approach to number assignment. The Agency Code field is statically assigned to a department, agency, or bureau through a registration process, and the assigned Agency Code values are listed in NIST SP 800-87. [SP800-87] The PIV Card Issuer for the registered department, agency, or bureau can, in turn, assign the System Code and Credential Number.

The FASC-N, as adopted and extended by FIPS 201, meets the objective of HSPD-12 to identify Federal employees and contractors. The success of the FIPS 201 technical standard has led other communities of interest to consider PIV-like identification systems. For some of these communities the FASC-N Identifier is not an appropriate solution since they are not agencies of the Federal government. Also, the data representation of the FASC-N was chosen for compatibility with deployed systems (fixed-length hexadecimal), and may not be optimal for binary identifier values prevalent in commercial systems today.

For these reasons, the CHUID data object also contains the GUID data element for future use. The GUID is a 16-byte, or 128-bit, binary field. It therefore improves on both the length and representation limitations of the FASC-N. Unfortunately, the GUID is only present in the CHUID, and does not serve to bind other data objects together. If the GUID were used to identify a PIV Card, the standard in effect would still require the FASC-N in the other data objects.

These issues lead to a number of questions. If a community outside the Federal government adopts PIV-like technology, what identifier format, registrar, and governance structure should they use? How could larger, binary identifiers be used with PIV-like technology? Could existing, standardized universal identifiers such as the Universal Unique Identifier (UUID), Internet Protocol version 6 (IPv6) addresses, OpenID identifiers, or Object Identifiers (OIDs) be used in place of the FASC-N, in all of its uses? If non-Federal-government communities adopt identifiers other than the FASC-N, could FIPS 201 be modified to recognize multiple types of identifiers?

> **Recommendation:** Agencies should collaborate to standardize an enhancement or replacement of the FASC-N that accomplishes both credential identification and object binding, and supports an extensible framework for subject identification.

10.2 Secure Biometric Match-On-Card

FIPS 201 defines the biometric authentication mechanisms BIO and BIO-A. According to these definitions, the PIV reference template object is stored on the PIV Card during issuance. When a PIV Card is inserted into a contact biometric reader and the PIN has been entered, the biometric reader can read the reference template object from the PIV Card. The subject presents a finger to a fingerprint scanner on the biometric reader, and the reader acquires a sample template from the scan. The reader then performs the matching algorithm comparing the reference and sample templates, and produces a Yes or No response. This is known as Match-Off-Card biometric authentication.

Biometric Match-On-Card is similar, but performs the match on the PIV Card instead of on the reader. To do this, the sample template must be sent to the reader, but the reference template need not leave the PIV Card. Secure Biometric Match-On-Card combines Biometric Match-On-Card with a secure communication protocol that encrypts the sample template as transmitted into the PIV Card, and signs a Yes or No result returned to the reader.

Secure Biometric Match-On-Card (SBMOC) has important benefits over Match-Off-Card. Communication of sensitive biometric data is always encrypted and can be decrypted only by the PIV Card. The subject's reference template is never released from the PIV Card. The biometric match is performed in the trusted execution environment of the PIV Card. ISO/IEC 7816 secure messaging commands and asymmetric cryptography mean that only the PIV Card can decrypt the biometric data and sign the result. [ISO/IEC7816] Moreover, the cardholder PIN is not required to perform the transaction. Because of the secure communication protocol and no PIN requirement, SBMOC can be performed safely and quickly over a contactless interface. Finally, because the match is performed on the PIV Card, the card knows and can use the result of the match.

NIST recently completed the Secure Biometric Match-On-Card Feasibility Study, as reported in NISTIR 7452 [SBMOC] and the companion MINEX II report [MINEXII]. The results of the SBMOC study show 17 cards successfully implemented the functionality and security requirements of the study, and met the 2.5 second transaction time goal. The MINEX II results indicate that one of the tested cards approached the accuracy of ANSI 378 matching algorithms, thereby exceeding the accuracy requirements of FIPS 201 as defined in [SP800-76]. Three additional smart cards and Match-On-Card algorithms met some, but not all, of the criteria.

> **Recommendation:** SBMOC should be pursued as a standard FIPS 201 authentication mechanism, especially for PACS. Assuming it is judged to be at least as trustworthy as PIN entry, SBMOC should be allowed to substitute for PIN to activate a PIV Card.

Appendix A—Recommendations

Section 2.2

> **Recommendation:** The OMB Memorandum [M-08-01] requires that the credential issuance be accomplished by October 27, 2008 (or by the date specified in the implementation plan mutually agreed-upon by the agency and OMB). Agency implementation plans should be written to accomplish the goals of HSPD-12.

Section 2.3

> **Recommendation:** This document recommends a risk-based approach for selecting appropriate PIV authentication mechanisms to manage physical access to Federal government facilities and assets. Agencies should seek recommendations on PACS architectures, authorization, and facility protection from other sources.

Section 4.9

> **Recommendation:** This section emphasizes the technical risks that remain with the CHUID authentication mechanism. If the CHUID authentication mechanism were implemented without restriction, operational risk would increase as the value of targets and the availability of cloning and counterfeiting tools increase. NIST therefore recommends that the CHUID authentication mechanism be implemented in only two situations: 1) access control points separating two areas at the same impact level, either Controlled or Limited; and 2) combined with the VIS authentication mechanism at access points between Unrestricted and Controlled areas. See Section 7 for further detail. NIST further recommends that the asymmetric CAK authentication mechanism be used instead of the CHUID authentication mechanism to the greatest extent practical.

Section 6.1

> **Recommendation:** To obtain the full benefit of PIV interoperability, HSPD-12 project managers should ensure that relying systems have the capability to use all cryptographic algorithms that apply to the authentication mechanism(s) performed. Departments and agencies should procure and deploy HSPD-12 products on the GSA HSPD-12 Evaluation Program Approved Products List where applicable, and can use the PIMM presented in Section 9 to measure progress toward the goal of interoperability. [FIPS 201 Evaluation Program]

Section 6.2

> **Recommendation:** Once all appropriate authentication mechanisms are satisfied, all access control decisions are made by comparing the 14 decimal digit FASC-N Identifier, and optionally the values of additional FASC-N fields, against the ACL entries.

> **Recommendation:** As agencies develop risk-based implementation plans, they will create and evolve plans for PIV Card issuance and application integration. They might consider which of the eight qualities are most relevant to agency goals and priorities, and derive further project objectives, metrics, and milestones from those qualities. They should also consider the relation of HSPD-12 to FISMA

requirements, and examine the potential for cost tradeoffs where PIV can replace more expensive authentication methods.

Section 6.3

Recommendation: Operational metrics should be designed to measure actual benefits over the operational lifetime of the PIV System. They may be derived by formulating each of the expected benefits above as a service quality metric, e.g., for "integrated system", service quality could be defined as the fraction of PACS registrations that are performed automatically by provisioning from the PIV issuance system.

Section 6.4

Recommendation: Maximum benefit will be obtained from the PIV System when it is adequately supported by infrastructure. Infrastructure upgrades may be justified, especially to improve communication among PACS system elements (e.g., support two way communication).

Section 7.1

Recommendation: NIST strongly recommends that every PIV Card contain an asymmetric CAK and corresponding certificate, and that PACS use an asymmetric challenge/response CAK protocol.

Recommendation: PACS should *always* verify the digital signature on the biometric template data object, and do path validation, before performing a match. Otherwise, the result of the match should not be trusted.

Recommendation: Biometric readers, especially those used at access points to Limited and Exclusion areas, should have a proven capability to accept live fingers and reject artificial fingers. Biometric readers, especially unattended readers in an Unrestricted area, should be physically hardened to protect against direct electrical compromise.

Section 7.3

Recommendation: Authentication assurance will be increased if a PACS uses relevant information from previous access control decisions ("context") when making a new access control decision. For example, if a cardholder attempts to pass from a Controlled to a Limited area, the PACS could require that the cardholder was recently allowed access to the Controlled area. Historically, rigorous implementation of this concept required person-traps and exit tracking, but partial implementations have significant value, and could be strengthened by new technology and systems integration.

Section 7.4

Recommendation: When a PIV Card is terminated, the PCI must revoke all valid authentication certificates for the PIV Card. The authentication certificates include the PIV Authentication Key certificate and the Card Authentication Key certificate (if present).

Recommendation: The CHUID may be collected at registration, but it should be treated as if it were a password for purposes of retention, i.e., hashed, the hash stored, and the CHUID deleted. A stored CHUID presents risks similar to a stored password; it can be copied and used to gain access. Data elements may be extracted from the CHUID and retained (e.g., the FASC-N, DUNS Number, and GUID), and a retained hash is sufficient to enable verification. *NIST strongly recommends against the storage of complete CHUIDs in relying systems.*

Recommendation: PKI and asymmetric CAK authentication mechanisms should be implemented by a PACS reader capable of full certificate path validation, either on-line or using a caching status proxy. Agencies should consider using on-line status checks as a means to reduce the latency of PIV Card status when a PIV Card is used for access to Exclusion areas. If a caching status proxy is used, the certificates should be captured when the PIV Card is registered to the PACS.

Section 7.5

Recommendation: On-line credential validation should be implemented for all of the FIPS 201 authentication mechanisms whenever possible. It is especially important when the one-factor, non-biometric mechanisms (CHUID, CAK) are used, because they could be exploited by simple possession of a misappropriated PIV Card. Caching techniques can be used to implement credential validation when on-line, on-demand credential validation is not possible. It is also recommended that the cached data be protected against tampering.

Recommendation: Path validation should be performed on all signed data objects required by the authentication mechanism in use. Path validation should employ on-line credential validation where possible, or cached certificate status where on-line certificate validation is not possible.

Section 8.6

Recommendation: Because having on-card role and permission information would raise difficult challenges concerning update and revocation, PACS permissions should generally be stored in a PACS facilities-based component, such as a panel or controller database.

Section 10.1

Recommendation: Agencies should collaborate to standardize an enhancement or replacement of the FASC-N that accomplishes both credential identification and object binding, and supports an extensible framework for subject identification.

Section 10.2

Recommendation: SBMOC should be pursued as a standard FIPS 201 authentication mechanism, especially for PACS. Assuming it is judged to be at least as trustworthy as PIN entry, SBMOC should be allowed to substitute for PIN to activate a PIV Card.

Appendix B—PIV Uniqueness

All access control decisions are made by comparing a FASC-N Identifier, which includes Agency Code, System Code, and Credential Number, against the ACL entries. Optionally, the values of additional FASC-N fields may also be compared. An ACL pattern may match the entire FASC-N, just the Agency Code, or the Agency Code and System Code (e.g., all PIV Cards issued to one agency, or to one site in one agency) without introducing dangerous collisions or ambiguities across agencies. In other words, an individual's FASC-N Identifier is unique among all cardholders when the complete three element subset of the FASC-N is used for comparison. There will be no collisions since all the cardholders have been assigned unique numbers.

This restricts the access control comparison to one of three cases:

1. the Agency Code alone (i.e., all PIV Cards with the same Agency Code are accepted);

2. the Agency Code and System Code only (i.e., all PIV Card with the same Agency Code and System Code are accepted); or

3. the Agency Code, System Code, and Credential Number (i.e., a uniquely identified PIV Card).

Any of these cases may also include comparison of additional FASC-N values such as the Credential Series, Individual Credential Issue, Organizational Identifier, or Person Identifier.

The FASC-N data fields are defined as fixed length values of Binary Coded Decimal digits. The complete subset of three data fields is 14 decimal digits in length, as stored on the PIV Card. Other representations of the FASC-N Identifier, for example a binary representation, may be used off-card, provided that they are isomorphic with respect to pattern matching. The following examples demonstrate the possible uses of FASC-N in a PIV-enabled PACS application.

B.1   Full FASC-N Comparison

The following table shows a successful match against an ACL pattern consisting of a full FASC-N comparison. These examples show an organization-specific access control policy that includes the comparison of all FASC-N fields.

FIELD NAME	PIV Card FASC-N	ACL FASC-N Pattern
Agency Code	3728	3728
System Code	8377	8377
Credential Number	123456	123456
Credential Series	1	1
Individual Credential Issue	1	1
Person Identifier	1234567890	1234567890
Organizational Category	1	1
Organizational Identifier	0010	0010
Person/Organization Association Category	1 1	

The following table shows an unsuccessful match against an ACL pattern consisting of full FASC-N comparison.

FIELD NAME	PIV Card FASC-N	ACL FASC-N Pattern
Agency Code	3728	3728
System Code	8377	8377
Credential Number	123456	234567
Credential Series	1	1
Individual Credential Issue	1	1
Person Identifier	1234567890	1234567890
Organizational Category	1	1
Organizational Identifier	0010	0010
Person/Organization Association Category	1 1	

B.2   FASC-N Identifier Comparison

The following table shows a successful match against an ACL pattern consisting of one specific FASC-N Identifier.

FIELD NAME	PIV Card FASC-N	ACL FASC-N Pattern
Agency Code	3728	3728
System Code	8377	8377
Credential Number	123456	123456

The following table shows an unsuccessful match against an ACL pattern consisting of one specific FASC-N Identifier.

FIELD NAME	PIV Card FASC-N	ACL FASC-N Pattern
Agency Code	3728	3728
System Code	8367	8377
Credential Number	123456	123456

B.3   Partial FASC-N Comparison

The following table shows a successful match against an ACL pattern consisting of an Agency Code and the System Code. The "x" symbols represent "don't care" decimal digits.

FIELD NAME	PIV Card FASC-N	ACL FASC-N Pattern
Agency Code	3728	3728
System Code	8391	8391
Credential Number	654321	xxxxxx

The following table shows an unsuccessful match against an ACL pattern consisting of an Agency Code and the System Code.

FIELD NAME	PIV Card FASC-N	ACL FASC-N Pattern
Agency Code	3628	3728
System Code	8377	8377
Credential Number	123456	xxxxxx

The following table shows a disallowed pattern that is not an initial string of the FASC-N Identifier.

FIELD NAME	PIV Card FASC-N	ACL FASC-N Pattern
Agency Code	3728	37xx
System Code	8377	83xx
Credential Number	123456	xxxxxx

B.4   Isomorphic FASC-N Comparison

The following table shows a successful match against an ACL pattern, with the FASC-N Identifier and the upper and lower bounds of the ACL pattern represented in hexadecimal. The match succeeds because the presented FASC-N Identifier is in the closed interval [LB, UB]. This example is the same as the MATCH example of B.2, with a shift in representation from decimal to hexadecimal.

FIELD VALUE	PIV Card FASC-N	ACL Pattern LB	ACL Pattern UB
Hexadecimal Value	21E9E156BBB1	21E9DBE03300	21E9E1D613FF

The following table shows an unsuccessful match against an ACL pattern, with the FASC-N Identifier and the upper and lower bounds of the ACL pattern represented in hexadecimal. The match fails because the presented FASC-N Identifier is not in the closed interval [LB, UB]. This example is the same as the NO MATCH example of B.2, with a shift in representation from decimal to hexadecimal.

FIELD VALUE	PIV Card FASC-N	ACL Pattern LB	ACL Pattern UB
Hexadecimal Value	21010BD3F280	21E9DBE03300	21E9E1D613FF

Appendix C—Possible PIV Authentication Mechanisms in PACS

The following list provides a complete list of possible PIV authentication mechanism combinations that are available for application to Federal facilities. The table entry contains PIV authentication mechanisms used to cross from Unrestricted to Controlled to Limited to Exclusion. The following acronyms are used in the table:

CV – CHUID + VIS

CAK – Card Authentication Key

BIO – Biometric

BIO-A – Biometric in Attendance

PKI – PIV Authentication Key

CPB – CAK + BIO combined or CAK + BIO-A combined

The table below provides all possible applications of PIV authentication mechanisms, progressing from Unrestricted to Exclusion areas. Note that the table includes individual PIV authentication mechanisms except for the combination of CV and CPB. Other PIV authentication mechanisms combinations can also be derived. The arrows in the above table represent the possibility of crossing multiple levels at an Access Point. For example, the arrow on Line 6 shows that CPB may be used to access Limited or Exclusion areas.

	Access Point A (Controlled)	Access Point B (Limited)	Access Point C (Exclusion)
1	CV BIO		PKI
2	CV BIO		CPB
3	CV BIO-A		PKI
4	CV BIO-A		CPB
5	CV PKI		BIO-A
6	CV CPB		→
7	CV CPB		BIO-A
8	CV CPB		PKI
9	CV CPB		CPB
10	CAK BIO		PKI
11	CAK BIO		CPB
12	CAK BIO-A		PKI
13	CAK BIO-A		CPB
14	CAK PKI		BIO-A
15	CAK CPB		→
16	CAK CPB		BIO-A
17	CAK CPB		PKI
18	CAK CPB		CPB
19	BIO BIO-A		PKI
20	BIO BIO-A		CPB
21	BIO PKI		→
22	BIO PKI		BIO-A
23	BIO PKI		PKI
24	BIO PKI		CPB

	Access Point A (Controlled)	Access Point B (Limited)	Access Point C (Exclusion)
25	BIO CPB		→
26	BIO CPB		BIO-A
27	BIO CPB		PKI
28	BIO CPB		CPB
29	BIO-A	→	PKI
30	BIO-A	→	CPB
31	BIO-A BIO PKI		
32	BIO-A BIO CPB		
33	BIO-A PKI →		
34	BIO-A PKI BIO-A		
35	BIO-A PKI PKI		
36	BIO-A PKI CPB		
37	BIO-A CPB →		
38	BIO-A CPB BIO-A		
39	BIO-A CPB PKI		
40	BIO-A CPB CPB		
41	PKI	→	BIO-A
42	PKI	→	CPB
43	PKI BIO		BIO-A
44	PKI BIO		PKI
45	PKI BIO		CPB
46	PKI BIO-A		→
47	PKI BIO-A		BIO-A
48	PKI BIO-A		PKI
49	PKI BIO-A		CPB
50	PKI PKI		BIO-A
51	PKI PKI		CPB
52	PKI CPB		→
53	PKI CPB		BIO-A
54	PKI CPB		PKI
55	PKI CPB		CPB
56	CPB	→	→
57	CPB BIO		BIO-A
58	CPB BIO		PKI
59	CPB BIO		CPB
60	CPB BIO-A		→
61	CPB BIO-A		BIO-A
62	CPB BIO-A		PKI
63	CPB BIO-A		CPB
64	CPB PKI →		
65	CPB PKI		BIO-A
66	CPB PKI		PKI
67	CPB PKI		CPB
68	CPB CPB		→
69	CPB CPB		BIO-A
70	CPB CPB		PKI
71	CPB CPB		CPB

The table below provides the effect of combination of PIV authentication mechanisms. The entry in the box corresponds to the result achieved after combination of two mechanisms represented in the row and column. For example, when PKI is combined with BIO the result is the same as CPB. The table below can be summarized as follows:

+ When CAK is combined with CV, the result is equivalent to CAK.

+ When BIO is combined with CV, the result is equivalent to BIO-A.

+ When PKI or CAK is combined with BIO or BIO-A, the result is equivalent to CPB.

+ When PKI is combined with CV or CAK, the result is equivalent to PKI.

+ When CPB is combined with any other PIV authentication mechanism, the result is equivalent to CPB.

	CV	CAK	BIO	BIO-A	PKI	CPB
CV						
CAK	CAK					
BIO	BIO-A	CPB				
BIO-A	BIO-A	CPB	BIO-A			
PKI	PKI	PKI	CPB	CPB		
CPB	CPB	CPB	CPB	CPB	CPB	

Appendix D—References

[FIPS199] Federal Information Processing Standard 199, Standards for Security Categorization of Federal Information and Information System, February 2004. See <http://csrc.nist.gov/>.

[FIPS201] Federal Information Processing Standard 201-1, Change Notice 1, Personal Identity Verification (PIV) of Federal Employees and Contractors, March 2006. See <http://csrc.nist.gov/>.

[FISMA] Federal Information Security Management Act of 2002. See <http://csrc.nist.gov/policies/HR2458-final.pdf>.

[FIPS 201 Evaluation Program] See <http://fips201ep.cio.gov/index.php>.

[HSPD-12] Homeland Security Presidential Directive 12, Policy for a Common Identification Standard for Federal Employees and Contractors, August 27, 2004.

[ISO/IEC7816] ISO/IEC 7816 (Parts 3, 4, 5, 6, 8, and 9), Information technology — Identification cards — Integrated circuit(s) cards with contacts.

[ISO/IEC14443] ISO/IEC 14443 (Parts 1, 2, 3, and 4):2000 Identification cards - Contactless integrated circuit(s) cards – Proximity cards.

[M-04-04] OMB Memorandum M-04-04, E-Authentication Guidance for Federal Agencies, December 2003. See <http://www.whitehouse.gov/omb/memoranda/fy04/m04-04.pdf>.

[M-05-24] OMB Memorandum M-05-24, Implementation of Homeland Security Presidential Directive 12—Policy for a Common Identification Standard for Federal Employees and Contractors, August 2005. See <http://www.whitehouse.gov/omb/memoranda/fy2005/m05-24.pdf>.

[M-08-01] OMB Memorandum M-08-01, HSPD-12 Implementation Status, October 2007. See <http://www.whitehouse.gov/omb/memoranda/fy2008/m08-01.pdf>.

[MINEXII] NIST Interagency Report 7477, Performance of Fingerprint Match-on-Card Algorithms, Phase II Report, February 2008. See <http://fingerprint.nist.gov/minexII/minex_report.pdf >

[PHYSEC] Field Manual 3-19.30. *Physical Security*. Headquarters, Department of the Army, United States of America. 8 January 2001.

[SBMOC] NIST Interagency Report 7452, Secure Biometric Match-on-Card Feasibility Report, November 2007.

[SECTION508] 1998 Amendment to Section 508 of the Rehabilitation Act, 29 U.S.C. ' 794d, see <www.section508.gov>.

[SKIMMER] How to Build a Low-Cost, Extended-Range RFID Skimmer, Ilan Kirschenbaum and Avishai Wool, Proceedings of the 15th Conference on USENIX Security Symposium - Volume 15. Vancouver, B.C., Canada. 8 May 2006.

[SP800-73] NIST Special Publication 800-73 Revision 2, Interfaces for Personal Identity Verification, September 2008.

[SP800-76] NIST Special Publication 800-76 Revision 1, Biometric Data Specification for Personal Identity Verification, January 2007.

[SP800-78] NIST Special Publication 800-78 Revision 1, Cryptographic Algorithms and Key Sizes for Personal Identity Verification, August 2007.

[SP800-79] NIST Special Publication 800-79 Revision 1, Guidelines for the Accreditation of Personal Identity Verification (PIV) Card Issuers (PCI's), June 2008.

[SP800-87] NIST Special Publication 800-87 Revision 1, Codes for the Identification of Federal and Federally-Assisted Organizations, April 2008.

[TIG SCEPACS] PACS v2.2, *Technical Implementation Guidance: Smart Card Enabled Physical Access Control Systems*, Version 2.2, The Government Smart Card Interagency Advisory Board's Physical Security Interagency Interoperability Working Group, July 27, 2004. (see http://www.smart.gov/information/TIG_SCEPACS_v2.2.pdf)

Appendix E—Abbreviations and Acronyms

ACL   Access Control List

ANSI   American National Standards Institute

BIO Biometrics

BIO-A Biometrics   with Attendant

BIO (-A)   a short-hand to represent both BIO and BIO-A authentication mechanism

BIO-O Biometric   Match-On-Card

CAK   Card Authentication Key

CCA Clinger-Cohen   Act

CHUID   Cardholder Unique Identifier

COOP   Continuity of Operations

CPB   Combination of CAK + BIO (-A) Authentication Mechanism

CPIC   Capital Planning and Investment Control

CRL   Certificate Revocation List

CV   a short-hand to represent CHUID + VIS authentication mechanism

DHS   Department of Homeland Security

DoD   Department of Defense

DOJ   Department of Justice

DUNS   Data Universal Numbering System

ECDSA   Elliptic Curve Digital Signature Algorithm

FASC-N   Federal Agency Smart Credential Number

FIPS   Federal Information Processing Standards

FISMA   Federal Information Security Management Act

FSL   Facility Security Level

GSA   General Services Administration

GUID   Global Unique Identifier

HSPD   Homeland Security Presidential Directive

ID Identification

IEC International   Electrotechnical Commission

IPv6   Internet Protocol version 6

ISO   International Organization for Standardization

IT Information   Technology

ITL Information   Technology Laboratory

LB Lower   Bound

NIST   National Institute of Standards and Technology

OCSP	Online Certificate Status Protocol
OID Object	Identifier
OMB	Office of Management and Budget
PACS	Physical Access Control System
PC Personal	Computer
PCI	PIV Card Issuer
PIMM	PIV Implementation Maturity Model
PIN	Personal Identification Number
PIV	Personal Identity Verification
RF Radio	Frequency
RSA	Rivest, Shamir, Aldeman
SBMOC	Secure Biometric Match-On-Card
SKI Symmetric	Key Infrastructure
SP Special	Publication
SSA	Social Security Administration
TCO	Total Cost of Ownership
UB Upper	Bound
UUID	Universal Unique Identifier
VIP	Very Important Person
VIS Visual	Inspection